CLASSIC REPRINT

A CRICKETER'S BOOK
1922

by Neville Cardus

FOREWORD

This book was originally published almost a century ago in hardback format and copies are now almost impossible to find.

We have therefore decided to produce a new edition of this book as part of our "Classic Reprint" series to go alongside our football titles. We know many customers follow both football and cricket and hope that this will be a popular addition to the series.

British Library Cataloguing in Publication Data
A catalogue record for this book is available from the British Library

ISBN: 978-1-86223-459-8

Copyright © 2021, SOCCER BOOKS LIMITED

72 St. Peter's Avenue, Cleethorpes, N.E. Lincolnshire, DN35 8HU, United Kingdom

Telephone   01472 696226

Web site   www.soccer-books.co.uk
e-mail   info@soccer-books.co.uk

All rights are reserved. No part of this publication may be reproduced, stored in a retrieval system or transmitted, in any form or by any means, electronic, mechanical, photocopying, recording, or otherwise, without the prior written permission of Soccer Books Limited.

Printed in the UK by 4edge Ltd.

A
CRICKETER'S BOOK

BY
NEVILLE CARDUS
("Cricketer" of "The Manchester Guardian")

WITH AN INTRODUCTION BY
A. C. MACLAREN

LONDON
GRANT RICHARDS LTD.
1922

CONTENTS

		PAGE
PREFACE	. . . .	vii
INTRODUCTION BY A. C. MACLAREN	. . .	ix

PART I—AT RANDOM

CHAPTER		
I.	THE GREATEST TEST MATCH . .	1
II.	THE SENSE OF PROPORTION . .	11
III.	AN OLD ENGLAND PLAYER . . .	16
IV.	FIRST PRINCIPLES IN BOWLING . .	24
V.	THE GAME IN KENT	29
VI.	"W. G."	85
VII.	LORD'S IN WET WEATHER . . .	42
VIII.	TOM RICHARDSON	45
IX.	TWO WONDERFUL BOYS . . .	51
X.	THE RETURN OF CRICKET . . .	59
XI.	ON TAKING A GAME TOO SERIOUSLY .	64
XII.	HOBBS	69
XIII.	JOHNNY BRIGGS	75
XIV.	LESSONS FROM LORD'S . . .	80
XV.	EVOLUTIONS	87
XVI.	COOK OF LANCASHIRE . . .	94
XVII.	THE FASHIONABLE BOWLING . .	100
XVIII.	TOM HAYWARD	105
XIX.	SPOONER AT OLD TRAFFORD . .	109
XX.	RHODES	112

CONTENTS

CHAPTER		PAGE
XXI.	Parkin and His Bowling	118
XXII.	William Gunn	123
XXIII.	Alec Watson	127
XXIV.	M. A. Noble	131
XXV.	The Cricketer as Artist	135

PART II—THE TEST MATCHES 1921

I.	Nottingham	143
II.	Lord's	156
III.	Leeds	174
IV.	Manchester	196
V.	The Oval	208

PART III—OF AUSTRALIANS

I.	Armstrong and the Australian Game	227
II.	The Australians—Gregory	232
III.	The Australians—Bardsley and Macartney	238
IV.	Impressions from Lord's — June 1921	244
V.	The Defeat at Eastbourne	249

PREFACE

SOME of the chapters in this book were written during the cricket seasons of 1919—21, and though they are now reprinted with, I trust, their periods polished more or less, every turn of phrase likely to relate them definitely to the events and to the time which provoked them has been left unaltered. My view is that writing on cricket tends to read coldly if it gives the impression that the writer has had to delve for his matter into the remote past. I have therefore used a day-by-day commentary on cricket of the last few summers, hoping by this " diary " method to give the reader a sense that my book was made while events still pricked all of us to enthusiasm. Such a method, no doubt, breeds inconsistencies. But if I have purchased even a little spontaneity at the cost of all the consistency an average cricketer's nature is capable of, I have surely made a good bargain. Cricketers are not, as a rule, fellows of hard logic, and I am content to fling the contradictions in my book on their mercy, pleading in extenuation that my ardour for cricket has not made at all easy the kind of canny judgment which looks warily behind and warily ahead before committing itself. My book, I am afraid, is the book of one who has loved the summer game rather irrationally.

PREFACE

Most of the chapters are based on articles which appeared in the *Manchester Guardian*, to whose Editor I am grateful for permission to make use of them here. Also I am grateful to the Editor of *The Nation* for permission to reprint the article called " The Cricketer as Artist."

INTRODUCTION

By A. C. MacLaren

It gives me much pleasure to write a little introduction to this book on cricket by Mr Neville Cardus. I have enjoyed it through and through, because it is the writing of a man who loves the game and whose touch is as delightful as his judgment is sound. When one reads him in the armchair one is transported to the ground and sees the game again in actual progress. The book takes the broadest survey of cricket. We glance back even to Hambledon; we see the great giants of the time of " W. G."; we have the game as it is on the village green as well as at Lord's; and it is not only our sporting interest in cricket that Mr Cardus quickens, but cricket's great beauty and charm and humour.

I think Mr Cardus was the only accredited journalist who did me the compliment of attending the first day of the Amateurs' Match at Eastbourne last summer, when the Australians suffered their first defeat. There were strong counter-attractions on the same day in London which it was the duty of all cricket journalists to attend—Surrey and Middlesex were fighting for the championship—and after the dreadful collapse of my XI. in the first innings Mr Cardus had to stand a lot of chaff for his long

INTRODUCTION

journey from Manchester to see so little! But the laugh was on his side at the finish.

To a very large extent he appears to share my views on the lack of success of our players generally in the Test matches, and on the apparent failure of the Selection Committee quite to place their fingers on the weak spots of the team—spots rendered beyond repair, possibly, by the unfortunate mishaps to Hobbs and Hearne. We were in the circumstances beaten by a better side, which played cricket as it should be played, and rather than " cut up " the Selection Committee—Selection Committees can never please everybody—it is more seemly to doff our hats to our gallant opponents and to thank them for the lessons they taught us last summer. And if anything can help us to get solace out of our failures I think Mr Cardus' book is likely to do so, with its enthusiasm and affection for the great summer game. And I have no doubt, in spite of everything, that English cricket to-day is worth all the fine writing it can get, and that we have plenty of young players promising splendid things for the future.

Eastbourne, April 1922.

PART I
AT RANDOM

" Pour on us torrents of light, good Sun,
Shine in the hearts of my cricketers, shine! "

CHAPTER I

THE GREATEST TEST MATCH

ON a bright day last spring I went to Lord's, hoping to see the first practice of the Australians. But the place was deserted, save for the man at the gates. He told me Armstrong's men were being entertained that afternoon somewhere in the City, and that they wouldn't be in the nets till after tea. Still, he added, with a touch of human nature not too common at Lord's, if I liked I could go in the ground and sit and enjoy myself in the sun till they came.

I sat on a bench with my feet spread out so that they touched the soft grass. A great calm was over the field. The trees beyond the "nursery" were delicate with fresh green, and the fine old pavilion seemed to nod in the sunshine. It was an occasion for a reverie, and I fell to affectionate thoughts upon the great days of cricket, of the history that had been made on the field which stretched before me. I thought of Grace, of Spofforth, of Hornby, of A. G. Steel. . . . Maybe I dozed for a while. Then I was conscious of a voice. "Would you mind moving up a little? This seat is rather congested." I looked around and saw sitting by my side a man in a tight black coat which buttoned high on his chest. He had side whiskers and wore a low turned-down collar

A CRICKETER'S BOOK

and a light bowler hat. A handkerchief was showing from a breast pocket in his jacket. Not quite awake yet, I " moved up." " Thank you," said he. " I'm sorry I disturbed you. A nap carries one comfortably through a long wait at these matches. What a crowd there is ! " I looked round. I was in the middle of a big crowd indeed. In front of me sat a parson. He was reading the *Times.* I glanced over his shoulder and saw the headline : " Egyptian Campaign : Sir G. Wolseley's Despatch." The man at my side said, " Were you here yesterday, sir ? " and before I could reply added, " It was a considerable day's cricket, and the *Post* has an excellent account. Perhaps you've seen it ? " He handed me a copy of the *Morning Post,* and, thanking him, I took it. The paper was dated August 29, 1882. In a column headed " England v. Australia " I read that on the day before Australia had been dismissed for 63 by Barlow and Peate, and that England, captained by A. N. Hornby, had made in reply 101. Then I understood my situation. And what is more I now understood it without the slightest astonishment. Even the aspect of the ground, which told me it was Kennington Oval and not Lord's, did not embarrass me. It was enough that I was one of the crowd which was to witness the second day's cricket in the ninth Test match—the most famous Test match of all.

I gave the *Post* back to my companion in silence. " A considerable day's cricket indeed, sir," said the Parson. " But England ought to have made more runs. Our batting was distinctly mediocre—almost

THE GREATEST TEST MATCH

as bad as the Australians'." A loud cheer disturbed his argument. Down the pavilion steps walked the England Eleven in single file, led by Hornby. With him was W. G., and he passed along the field with an ambling motion, and the wind got into his great black beard. He spoke to Hornby in a high-pitched voice and laughed. Then he threw the ball to a tall, graceful player just behind him and cried, "Catch her, Bunny." Following Grace and Hornby were Lucas, C. T. Studd, J. M. Read, the Hon. A. Lyttleton, Ulyett, Barlow, W. Barnes, A. G. Steel and Peate. The crowd quietened, awaiting the advent of Australia's first two batsmen, and I again heard the Parson's voice. " . . . The English total was distressingly poor. Rarely have I seen poorer batting from an All England Eleven. The fact is, sir, that for some little time now English cricket has been deteriorating. Our batsmen don't hit the ball as hard as they used to do, and even our bowling . . ." Another cheer drowned his discourse. " Bannerman and Massie," said my companion. "I should imagine Bannerman's the youngest man in the match." The Parson was prompt with his correction. "I believe S. P. Jones, who was 21 on the 1st of the month, is the junior member of the two teams. Studd is, I fancy, eleven months older than Jones. Bannerman is 28 at least, and Giffen is six days younger than Bannerman." My companion was silenced, but I ventured a question. "How old is Spofforth?" Pat came the answer, "Twenty-seven on the ninth of next month."

The crowd, including even the Parson, went as quiet as a mouse as Barlow began the English bowling to Bannerman. Lyttelton, behind the wicket, crouched low. It was exactly a quarter past twelve. The next half-hour was a tumultuous prelude to the day. Bannerman was all vigilance, while Massie played one of the great innings of Test cricket. He hurled his bat at every ball the slightest loose, and his hits crashed ponderously to the boundary. He was the living image of defiance as he faced the Englishmen, glaring round the field his challenge. At one huge drive from Barlow's bowling my companion murmured, "I've never seen a bigger hit than that at the Oval." But the Parson overheard him. "When the Australians were here in '78," he said, "W. H. Game, playing for Surrey, hit a ball from Spofforth to square leg right out of the ground." Still, he admitted that this Massie fellow hit them quite hard enough. In half an hour England's advantage of 38 was gone. Hornby called up bowler after bowler, Studd for Barlow, Barnes for Studd. Steel tried his hand at 56—the sixth bowler in less than three-quarters of an hour. When Australia's score was 47 Massie lifted a ball to long on. "Lucas is there," said the Parson; "he'll get it all r—— Good Lord!" For Lucas dropped the ball and blushed red as the crowd groaned out of its very soul.

"Sixty-six for none," murmured the man at my side; "they're 28 on with all their wickets intact. If Massie prevails— ah, bravo, sir; well bowled, well bowled!" A ball from Steel had tempted Massie,

THE GREATEST TEST MATCH

and just as he jumped out broke back and wrecked the wicket. Massie walked to the pavilion, roared home by an admiring but much relieved crowd. His innings was worth 55 to Australia, made out of 66 in less than an hour.

Bonnor came next, and the English out-fields dropped deep and had apprehensive thoughts. Would not Massie's example make this bearded giant a very Jehu? But Hornby has an inspiration. He asks Ulyett to bowl instead of Steel. And Ulyett moves to the wicket like a man ploughing against a breaker, puts the last ounce of his Yorkshire strength into a thunderbolt of a ball that sends Bonnor's middle stump flying. The crowd is only just getting back the breath lost in approval of this feat when Bannerman is caught by Studd at extra mid-off. Bannerman has batted seventy minutes for 13. " Quick work for him ! " says the Parson. And with the broad bat of Bannerman out of the way the English bowlers begin to see daylight. Peate's slow left-handed deliveries spin beautifully, as though controlled by a string. The Australians now, save Murdoch, are just guessing. The fourth wicket falls at 75, the fifth at 79. Australia are all out 122. " Only 85 to win," says the Parson. " It's our game after all, though Lucas did his best to lose it."

It was a true autumn afternoon going to its fall in grey light when " W. G." and Hornby went to the wicket to face Spofforth and Garratt. The crowd filled the ground, but so silent was it as Grace took his guard that one could hear the tink-tink of a hansom cab coming closer and closer along the Vauxhall Road. Spofforth's first over was fast—he let the ball go with a quick leap, dropping his arm at the moment of release. Blackham "stood back" when Grace was batting, but crept up for Hornby. "Beautiful wicket-keeping," murmured my companion. "Pinder was not less gifted," said the Parson. And he added, "I have not seen Spofforth bowl as fast as this for a long time. He has latterly cultivated medium-pace variations." Both Hornby and Grace began confidently, and at once the tension lifted. Hornby made a lovely cut from Spofforth and a dainty leg stroke for a couple.

Spofforth uprooted Hornby's off stump with England's score 15, and with his next ball clean bowled Barlow. The crowd gave out a suspicion of a shiver, but the advent of bluff George Ulyett was reassuring, especially as Grace welcomed him with a fine leg hit from Garratt for three and a beautiful on drive to the boundary from Spofforth. "Thirty up," said my companion; "only 55 to get." England was still 30 for two when Spofforth crossed over to the pavilion end. Now I was behind his arm; I could see his superb break-back. And he bowled mainly medium pace this time. With each off break I could see his right hand, at the end of the swing over, finish near the left side, "cutting" under the ball. Sometimes his arm went straight over and continued straight down in the follow-through—and then the batsman had to tackle fierce top spin. There was the sense of the inimical in his aspect now.

THE GREATEST TEST MATCH

He seemed taller than he was a half-hour ago, and the right arm of him more sinuous. There was no excitement in him; he was, the Parson said, cold-blooded. Still, Ulyett faced him bravely while Grace, at the other end, time after time moved from his crease with a solid left leg and pushed the ball away usefully. "Fifty up," said my companion, "for two wickets. It's all over—we want only 84 now." And at 51 Spofforth bowled a very fast one to Ulyett, who barely snicked it. It served, though; Blackham snapped the catch, and his " Hzat ! " was hoarse and aggressive. Lucas came in, and with two runs more " W. G." was caught at mid-off. "What a stroke !" said the Parson. " I'm afraid he's not the Grace he was." Four for 53, and Lyttelton and Lucas in. Lyttelton hits out big-heartedly, but the field is like a net tightly drawn. It is suddenly understood by every man of us that the game is in the balance. " The wicket must be bad," says somebody.

Lucas stonewalls, with a bat as straight as a die. Spofforth bowls a maiden; Boyle bowls a maiden; Spofforth bowls another maiden. The air is growing thick. "Get runs or get out, for the Lord's sake," says somebody. The field creeps closer and closer to the wicket. Spofforth and Boyle are like uncanny automatons, bowling, bowling, bowling. . . . Six successive maidens. "This," says the Parson, " this is intolerable." One's heart is aching for an honest boundary hit. . . . And the human bowling machines send down six more successive maidens. Think of it; twelve successive maidens, and the game

A CRICKETER'S BOOK

in that state, the crowd in that purgatory. "When Grace was a boy of 18 I saw him make 50 on this very ground, and he played every ball he got." It was the Parson again, but now he sounded a little strained, a little unhappy. At the end of the twelfth successive maiden, a hit was purposely misfielded that Spofforth might have a " go " at Lyttelton. The batsmen fell into the snare. Four more maidens, and spinning is Lyttelton's wicket. "Anyhow, that's over and done with ! " thankfully breathes the crowd. Better all be dead than dying ! England five for 66 —19 needed. Steel comes next and Lucas hits a boundary. Roars the crowd " Bravo ! " then catches breath.   Steel caught and bowled Spofforth none— Maurice Read clean bowled second ball.   England seven for 70. "Incredible ! " say 20,000 people in dismal unison. Barnes, the next man, hits a two. Thirteen to win. Heaven bless us, Blackham has blundered ! He allows three byes. Run Barnes, run Lucas ! Spofforth is inscrutable as the crowd makes its noises. His next ball is too fast for eyes at the boundary's edge to see. Lucas comes down on it, though—hard, determined. And the ball rolls ever so gently on to the off wicket and disturbs the bail. Poor Lucas bows his head and departs, and blasphemy is riot throughout the crowd and is communicated by stages to the outer darkness of Kennington Road. The stars are set against England—our cricketers are for the first time on English soil face to face with a victorious Australian XI. With ten to struggle after, Blackham catches Barnes off his glove,

THE GREATEST TEST MATCH

and the last man is here—poor Peate, who is the best slow bowler in England and not a bit more of a cricketer than that, and what good are his mysteries of spin now? Studd is there yet, though; only ten runs and it is our game. Perhaps *he*—Peate has hit a two. It was audacious, but maybe the ball was a safe one to tackle. A bad ball's a bad ball at any time. Peate has nerve (so we are telling ourselves, desperately): he's the right man: he'll play the steady game to good stuff and leave the job to Studd. . . . The stark truth is that Peate hit out wildly yet again at a slow from Boyle, missed it, and was bowled. There was a hollow laugh somewhere as the wicket went back, but whether it came from this world or the next I couldn't say. Studd did not get a ball. "Why, man, did you try to hit: why couldn't you just stop them?" they asked Peate. "Well," he replied, "I couldn't trust Maister Studd!"

As Peate's wicket was broken ten thousand people rushed the rails and hid the green field. Spofforth was carried shoulder-high to the pavilion, and there the mob praised a famous man. I, too, wanted to get up and shout, but somehow I was rooted to my seat. I was probably the only man in that multitude on the pavilion not standing up, and as I sat there I had a strange sense of making a lonely hole in a solid black mass. The Parson was standing on the seat beside me. His boots were not more than two feet from my eyes and I could see the fine ribbed work on the upper edge of the soles. The cheering came downwards to me, sounding remote. I lost grip on events. It seemed that I sat there till the ground was almost deserted, till over the field came a faint mist, and with it the vague melancholy of twilight in a great city. Time to go home, I thought . . . a great match . . . great days . . . great men . . . all gone . . . far away . . . departed glory . . . A hand of someone touched my shoulder and I heard him say: "The Orsetralians are on the way, and they'll be in the nets at four o'clock. Nice in the sun, isn't it?"

CHAPTER II

ON PRESERVING A SENSE OF PROPORTION

(Trent Bridge, May 1921)

On a notable Saturday in May there tramped over Trent Bridge the longest-faced crowd that ever lived, and it talked of the passing of English cricket. Great old masters of the game moved in the ranks, despondent as any of us. One of them, A. C. MacLaren, might well have rubbed salt in our wounds with a vile " I told you so." His was the credit of having foreseen England's downfall against Gregory and Macdonald months before, even in the hour of our fool's paradise, and as one saw him at Trent Bridge at the end of the first day of the first Test match discussing the remaining games, how keenly one might have given him Macbeth's

> . . . Say from whence
> You owe this strange intelligence? or why
> Upon this blasted heath you stop our way
> With such prophetic greeting?

For Trent Bridge was a blasted heath on this Saturday. The writer does not pretend that his spirits were livelier than anybody else's in the miserable crowd; on occasions such as these, in circumstances that are bludgeoning too crudely and plainly, Mark Tapleyism is abominable. The crowd acted rightly, considering the hour, and like Mr Povey in "The Old Wives' Tale," gave itself up unashamedly to affliction.

At the very fall of the same fateful day, the writer found himself on a quiet country field watching a cricket match that might have walked right out of Miss Mitford. The players were keen, and variously attired. Some of them were cricketers down to the waist only, and after that quite definitely artisans. Others, not content that they were " flannelled " all over, strained vanity farther and wore neckties. A little group of onlookers in front of a wooden pavilion contained a few of the oldest inhabitants of the district, and also two ruddy-faced housewives who sat on a bench and conducted some knitting diligently enough, yet sparing an amount of consciousness sufficient to maintain a point of contact with the cricket. They kept themselves aware of the game and its gradations towards stages of crisis rather as they would regard the kettle on the boil at home the while they went on with the ironing. Just as I came upon this little scene the district parson went out to bat. As he did so the housewives put down their knitting and concentrated upon him. That the parson should be playing cricket moved them quite plainly with the wonder and glory of life. The parson mowed a ball to the boundary agriculturally, and then was bowled middle-stump. " What a shame ! " said the housewives, and no doubt it was. The parson returned to the wooden pavilion, sat down and took off his pads. " It's no use," he said, " I can't play this game. I

ON PRESERVING A SENSE OF PROPORTION

like it, mind you, but I can't play it!" And in that simple utterance he revealed himself a true cricketer, and at the same time set working again in one of his listeners, at least, the sense of proportion.

By the time this rustic cricket match was over Trent Bridge and its horrors had passed like a nightmare. This simple cricket match, conducted by cricketers who couldn't play, but liked it, seemed to announce that the game is in as cheerful a way as ever it was in this country, that the true spirit of it is still quick enough. Because of Gregory, it seemed to declare, shall there be no more cakes and ale in our cricket field?

It is grand, of course, that there should be Test matches, and it is grievous that England should be at the moment overthrown at cricket. But it is worth remembering that only a few of us can play for England, and that our parson, with his " Derbyshire cut," would probably not be considered a cricketer at all by an England Eleven. Are we doing the right thing by the game to allow the Test matches, and the first-class game generally, to stand so totally for cricket in our minds, and to judge upon the condition of cricket at large from the happenings in these highly specialised centres? Who will sing the club game nowadays; who will point to Little Slocombe's victory over Old Puddleton in answer to the current cry " English cricket is decadent "? Never, surely, have we been in this country so much in danger as to-day of taking our cricket too seriously, through thinking too " imperially " of it! Cricketers here and there are playing " for safety " in the common day-by-day matches—playing a game untrue to themselves that they might be invited to play for England. The Australians are putting into the game a grimness that hardens the sunny nature of it. It is for them first and last a combative business—they have little use for the airs and graces of cricket, its summer pleasaunces, unless victory be in sight.

Did ever a cricketer get so much sheer antagonism into cricket as Macdonald, the Australian fast bowler, got into his bowling at Trent Bridge? His face was set to a quite pained grimness—a man in battle itself could wear no aspect more formidable. What would Hirst and Briggs have thought of it? The Australian game has never given us cricketers as lovable as these, though it has given us even greater men— for a combat. But were they the greater *cricketers*? The other day the writer talked with an old cricketer who played for England many years ago, and asked him if he could recall his happiest hour in the cricket field. " Aye," he said. " I was at Adelaide, fielding at ' cover ' one afternoon, and I saw the sun shining on the steeples of the churches outside the ground. It was a wonderful sight ! " No word about his spoils of battle. He spoke of his day in the sun, and remembered nothing of his acquaintance with cricket better than the beauty of it, the fun of it, and the fellowship in it. If you look to a game for the letting-off of combative energy go to football —it is the better game if you want combat pure and simple. There is time in football for little *but*

ON PRESERVING A SENSE OF PROPORTION

combat, no matter how skilful the antagonists. But in cricket there is time even to look at the churches in the sunshine at Adelaide—and in a Test match at that! The game finds room in it for more amenities than any other game in the world. At its best—that is, as they play it every Saturday afternoon at Little Slocombe—there is room in it even for a " duffer." Who has ever found for the man that misses a goal at football a term so indulgent and genial as " butter-fingers "? In what other game have such happy souls lived and expressed themselves as Tom Emmett, Hirst, Briggs, Albert Trott, and David Hunter? It will perhaps be as well to keep the large humanity of these cricketers in mind just now. They, at any rate, never sundered for a moment from " the club game," and never forgot that cricket is played to the passing of summer. And even if England should lose all the Test matches in a summer some day there will be no more significance about the issue than that England *has* lost all the Test matches. The parson on the little ground round about Trent Bridge will none the less have had his season of content—will still love the game, no matter how ill he has played it.

CHAPTER III

AN OLD ENGLAND PLAYER

I MET him in a village far from the noise of cities, a village in which it was easy to think that time had stood still and the land was the quiet and rather fragrant thing it was in the years of his fame. Now, in his old age, he performed for livelihood some mechanical duty in a hosiery factory, and as I looked on him working at his bench one dark December afternoon and saw his white hair and the spectacles down his nose, I thought sadly of his proud days in the sun. He would not at first talk of cricket when I sat with him in his cottage after his work was over. He pretended to me that never in his life had he been so comfortable as he now was. He even affected to believe that with his life to live again he would not be a professional cricketer. "It's no more'n a game," he said, " and in a lifetime at it you prodooce nowt ! " These were the sophistries it was necessary for him to cultivate, that he might not too sharply feel the pathos which age and faltering flesh bring to the cricketer whose love of the game to the end burns a bright light.

And love the game he did in his heart. His eyes began to flash as slowly I led him on to a talk over the old times. And, at last, the spell of memory

AN OLD ENGLAND PLAYER

began to work; he was back again in the 'eighties and 'nineties, England's great bowler, in the company of Tom Richardson, Lockwood, Peel, and Lohmann, with summer passing before him like a pageant. He spoke of Lord's, and recollected June mornings in London when he walked to the ground down the St. John's Wood Road, with polished magnificence of hansom cabs all about him. A day in the sun was before him, green grass for his young confident movements. In his period, Lord's was a different Lord's from the one we know. " I went there a summer or two ago," he said, " and I didn't know it. It was crowded and full o' noise. In my day folk didn't flock to cricket matches, and many's the time as I've played at Lord's [he pronounced it Loard's] and it's been nigh empty and that calm that you could hear the echo of a bat coming over the field. Hey! and the pavilion was a grand place; you were feared to breathe as you walked past all the fine gentry when you went out to bat." It is easy to imagine the scene he had in mind. Look into the Badminton cricket book and ponder that picture of the immaculates of the pavilion at Lord's in 1880. Shining tall hats imposing on you everywhere. True, one nobleman has his tall hat on his knees while he takes the air, but his tall hat being on his knees you can see and admire the better the classic cast of his forehead. Bone of the finest bone, flesh of the most exclusive flesh, is every scion of them. " There was some rare gentlemen and no mistake at Lord's in them times," said my old cricketer. " It did your eyes good to look at 'em, all shining like and mighty." I understood he did not consider the stock in the pavilion at Lord's nowadays to be so pure, and I am certain he thought the less of Lord's—just a little the less—on that account.

The wonder and glory of life are in the way my old cricketer first went to Lord's—a raw-boned lad now for the first time in his life out of his native village: one week an old widow's only son labouring obscurely on the soil, the next week bowling " from the nursery end," while the fashionable intelligence in the pavilion pronounced his name interestedly. " Th' old woman," he told me, meaning his mother, " was funny when I told her as I were going to play for th' county. ' I reckon nowt to that,' she said: ' th' village team's good enough for thee.' But I knowed she were glad in her heart, only she were feared as I'd get hurt playing for th' county. She allus were worryin' about that, and when I didn't get into t' England team in '93 when I was at th' top of my form she were reight sorry proper, but she made to believe she were glad. Somebody had been reading t' paper to her about Ernest Jones." In his great days he went on living in his quiet village with his mother, till she died. Can you see him, coming home some summer evening to their little cottage, after a day in a Test match amongst great men and in a great place, coming home and sitting quietly with her at supper in the lamp-light, and at that very moment his name notable in conversation all over the land?

AN OLD ENGLAND PLAYER

The county discovered his ability when he was playing on the waste land outside his village. One evening "a gentleman in a top-hat" spoke to him and asked for his name and address. A day or two later he was at the nets at the county ground, and in a week he was moving south with the county team, bound for Lord's to play against an M.C.C. XI. captained by Grace.

On the opening morning of the match he went to Lord's while his clubmates were sitting in the smoke-room of the hotel after breakfast. He hadn't the patience to wait for them: he *must* be "out and doing." "I walked up to th' big gates," he told me, "with my flannins [meaning flannels] in brown paper under my arm, but th' gatekeeper wouldn't let me in and I couldn't make out to him who I was. Then a big gentleman come up, and he had a great black beard. I knew it was th' old man, and he got me into th' ground. He'd heard about me, he said, when I spoke to him. 'Aye,' says he, 'Mr Johnson told me about you. So you're goin' to bowl us all out, eh? Well, I'm no good against a colt first time he bowls at me.'" And two hours later this rosy-faced lad was bowling at Grace. "Mr Johnson put me on after t' first hour, an' th' old man and Mr Ferris had put up a score for t' first wicket. I can see him now—his big body making t' wickets look so little that you felt t' ball weren't big enough to hit 'em. And when he kept putting his left leg down th' pitch and smothering th' ball—hey, I felt as helpless as a babby!" "W. G.'s" defence looked so impenetrable on the days he was in form that my old cricketer said Attewell used to say to the umpires, " Eh, but yoh ought to get th' gauge out and measure 'is bat. He meks 'em 'isself."

But not all the grand incidents of his career did my old cricketer recollect clearly. Sadly, I found his memory had failed to hold many a great moment's splendour. It was as though days and days had passed through him like water through a sieve. " Often I looks at Wisden's," he said, " and sees th' scores in matches as I played in, but I can hardly believe I was the same man when I finds mi name there." But there were things he would never, never forget. " Ranji ! " he said, " I s'll remember him till my dyin' day ! " He witnessed again, as he sat there looking into the fire, the dark grace of the man, the lithe body, the silk shirt fluttering in the breeze, his bat seemingly more supple than other cricketers' bats, making movements in curves so swift that you might easily imagine it was flexible, like a cane. On a fast wicket his first stroke told you that he was there for the afternoon. He flicked you anywhere he chose in the casual way a man flicks off a daisy's head with his stick. " When he come in to bat we all used to try and get 'is wicket first, for the pride o' the thing, and bowl us selves for all as we were worth. Then we sort of knew it would be no good. It come over you all of a sudden like, and I used to feel summat give inside me."

It was not Ranji, though, who was the bitter torment of the souls of bowlers in his time, but one

AN OLD ENGLAND PLAYER

name of Shrewsbury. He was past his best when this old man played the game, " and," said he, " when they told us that we used to thank the Lord for it." There was always a chance for the bowler tackling Ranji: even as he conjured your best length ball from the middle stump to the fine leg boundary you could hope on, grasping at the idea of human fallibility, telling yourself he would do it once too often. Besides, Ranji in one of his long innings would in time persuade even the bowlers into the magic circle of his art, and once there they were spellbound by his charm even as the crowd. It was different bowling at Shrewsbury; nothing here but naked antagonism, nothing for the poor bowler to think on but the toil of getting him out. On the hardest and most perfect turf he never strayed from the eternal verities of his art, and whether his score was none or 200 his play went on with the same cool scrupulousness, the same self-control. " His bat were all middle," said the old cricketer, " and even on a sticky wicket you couldn't make him look awkward."

Gunn and Shrewsbury at the wicket on a hot day, and how pitilessly bowlers were scourged! Lockwood and Richardson in action against their defences, hurling down the fastest that was in them as though by some great convulsion of nature, and in vain! When Notts won the toss in those days on a firm ground bowlers gave themselves over unashamedly to affliction; and if it was a match at Brighton the rest of the Notts men went down to the sea to bathe. To watch Gunn and Shrewsbury in partnership was to have a classical education in batsmanship. This period, my old cricketer's period, saw the classic style touch perfection. The rough grounds of the 'seventies and 'eighties had flawed the work of many a master perhaps not less gifted than Shrewsbury; but now the smooth wickets admitted the precision which is three parts of the classic manner. And not only was the batsmanship of the day flawlessly pure in style: bowling, too, had the same clarity of outline. Length, length, length! Poise and balance! The ball pitching on the mythical sixpenny-piece, the bowler making a beautiful movement. Even the fast bowlers had the classic rhythm, and none so beautiful as Richardson to look upon. It was the day of first principles, and in the cricket field Shrewsbury and Gunn and Attewell and my old cricketer announced the validity of them even as the Spencerian philosophers were announcing them to the workaday world outside. The age of rationalism, of men who disliked the oblique! Soon there were to come the first touches of decadence into cricket, the "rococo allurements" of Ranjitsinhji, his music drawing to ruin all the innocents of the field. But my old cricketer and the men he played with, though they heard the first call of the magic pipe, little dreamed of its significance. To the end of their cricketing days the straight bat and the honest length ball were enough for them. This old man showed me a worn cricket ball. "I clean bowled the Old Man, W. W. Read, and A. E. Stoddart in a couple of overs with that ball, on a plumb Oval wicket, and every ball of

AN OLD ENGLAND PLAYER

'em as straight as a whistle!" I took the ball in my hand and wondered if the fragrance of many a golden day was not in it somewhere.

And now I had to leave the old fellow. "Sorry to have to say good night to ye," he said, "but I mun see about putting on t' alarm clock for t' morning." As I left his cottage he was tinkering with the clock and setting it for 6.30. On my way home it so happened that the train passed the county cricket ground that had been the old man's heaven on earth. I peered through the carriage window-panes, but the field was hidden in the bitter December night, and it seemed that summer and cricket could never come there again.

CHAPTER IV

FIRST PRINCIPLES IN BOWLING

(*June* 1921)

THE Kent cricketer, W. J. Fairservice, has written a little booklet called "Hints on Bowling," in which he reminds us of one or two first principles of this art that nowadays are not quite fashionable. He clings to the notion—cultivated of old by men like Attewell and Shaw—that good length is "the main essential" in bowling. In recent years we have most of us had a secret contempt for the old school that pegged away on a given spot, trusting to an accurate pitch and just a little natural bias or nip from the wicket. We have talked loftily of the "evolution" of bowling, and boasted our ability to "turn them the wrong way." The man without finger spin in large quantities we have regarded as a Methuselah of the game. In a word, bowling has been forced into a fine decadence. Decadence always comes as soon as we fall in love with some technical dodge for its own sake, and overlook the purpose for which it was fashioned. The bowler's object is to get wickets—a commonplace that has gone into neglect simply because bowlers wholesale have fallen in love with spin for the glory of spin,—with the technical refinements

FIRST PRINCIPLES IN BOWLING

of bowling of these days. The fascination of this decadence is really difficult to set aside. What cricketer that has known the joy which comes of breaking a ball from the off with a leg-break action can resist the temptation to exploit the trick in season and out of season—aye, even if he knows a good straight-length ball would get his man out quicker?

To-day we are paying for over-indulgence in the spin and swerve luxuries. The note of modern bowling is inaccuracy of length. Our batsmen, not less than the bowlers themselves, have got into a loose way through the general disobedience of the old principle—length first, length always. Batsmanship, after waxing fat on half-volleys and long hops, is this summer made to look a weakling by Armstrong, simply because he bowls a good length. Consider his bowling figures—769 overs and five balls, 277 maidens, 1544 runs, 106 wickets—what an exposure is here of English batsmanship! In a season of perfect wickets, the slow leg-break bowler is hit for some mere two runs every six balls in 770 overs. How do they think of Armstrong's power over English cricketers in Australia? Is it not a fact that the " barrackers " there advise long on to move towards Toowoomba when Armstrong goes on to bowl? What does the laughter-loving Armstrong himself think, in the silence of the night, of his latter-day position at the top of the English bowling averages? Does he not shake the bed to a violent motion?

It is not his leg-break that has made our cricketers impotent before him, but just his superb length. (Maybe if he were not Armstrong the Australian captain, even his length would not so easily put scores of our batsmen into a catalepsy!) It has been suggested that Armstrong's leg-break is difficult because it is in effect the left-hander's most dangerous ball, the one that breaks away. But the contrast between the line of flight and the break in Armstrong's bowling is not as disconcerting as the contrast between flight and break in the left-hander's bowling. Armstrong breaks away after a direction through the air that does not, so to speak, contradict the spin's direction in advance. The left-hander's flight is in distinct contrast to his break, and the margin of error in playing the ball is, on the face of it, greater than with the break of Armstrong's ball. Armstrong's leg-break is " flighted " fairly straight (we are not discussing it as bowled conventionally—that is, outside the leg-stump; no subtlety lurks in that ball) and simply turns away: the left-hander's ball breaks away after it has taken a flight *into* the batsman's wicket. Playing a straight one from a Woolley—one that does not go away—will be harder to manage than the straight one from Armstrong.

All of which is not mere digression from the matter of length in bowling. If it proves that there is not the complication in Armstrong's work that some of the critics would have us believe, easier the job will be of showing that Armstrong's power consists in his length. The modern young man need not be scepti-

FIRST PRINCIPLES IN BOWLING

cal. Peate, a great slow bowler, admitted that it was accuracy of pitch that got him his wickets on hard grounds. "They say they break this way and that," he declared, "but it's length that does it." Shaw had no large amount of finger spin, nor had Attewell. They were "natural" bowlers, with no tricks of a cultivated order. Fairservice in his little book has put his finger, probably unknowingly, on what is perhaps the most pernicious consequence of an overdose of finger-spin. He says: "Body action is often responsible for causing the ball to break. By body action I mean the action the body goes through in preparation for delivering the ball and the actual delivery of the ball. Most bowlers use their bodies when bowling, but some only very little. Bowlers who do use their bodies are generally the best bowlers." How little of body action do a lot of modern spin bowlers get into their work! Surely they bowl almost entirely from the finger tips. The energy of the body certainly does not pass impetuously into the swing of the arm, as it goes over, if you are preoccupied with finger spin. As a consequence, a vast quantity of modern bowling has no strong life in its rise from the pitch—the spin is there, but the ball has not been propelled vigorously, and banged violently down to the ground. Of the great bowler one is able to say that the whole man bowls. His every ounce of energy goes into the work, the rhythm of his action is free and full. All the masters of length bowling had a body action. Perhaps they did not turn the ball as stupendously as it often is turned nowadays, but they turned it amply enough for their purposes. It may be that young bowlers in this country will learn the utility of first principles in bowling from the success of Armstrong's "old fashioned" ways. If that happens the Australians some day may have cause to think that they did not get the ashes for nothing in 1921.

CHAPTER V

THE GAME IN KENT

(June 1920)

IN Kent it is hard indeed to believe that cricket has its doubting Thomases—those who tell us the great summer pastime is passing away. I write these notes in an old-world inn a stone's-throw from the enchanting cricket ground at Tonbridge. The place is full of men who have dropped in for drinks on their way home from the first day of the Lancashire and Kent match, and the talk is of nothing else but cricket, cricket, cricket. And this very afternoon a race called the Royal Hunt Cup has been run; some horse has won and lost fortunes up and down the land. The event so far has certainly not impinged on the consciousness of this crowd downstairs, thirsty but voluble from a day in the sun on the Angel cricket field. Is it not something for a cricketer to have lived for—to find the old game given preference over " the horses " by the man in the street at his drinks?

Tonbridge, of course, is one of the cradles of the game. The cricket field on which Lancashire played Kent must have its great and honourable shades. For, long before the coming of the inventor of modern cricket—W. G. Grace—" the tall men of Kent " fought with bat and ball, in top-hats and braces, on this very Angel "middle," and surely Alfred Mynn was with them. Cricket is in the blood of every Kentish boy. There were scores of them at the Lancashire and Kent match, and outside the enclosure little urchins who could not "raise the wind" struggled to get up telegraph poles overlooking the field of play. Failing this, they took off their coats and themselves fought the great match in miniature, with primitive weapons and wickets chalked on the boards—and, I suspect, chalked by a bowler, intent on giving the bat a vast expanse to defend. These urchins aped the Kent county men; the biggest of them was "Woolley," but I could not gather whether "they made the baby Captain Hook"—in other words, whether they let the smallest undertake the part of the least famous cricketer in the county.

And not only are these things going on in Tonbridge to amaze and delight the cricketer from the North of England. Also is it "cricket week." Which means that the whole town, as soon as the day's work is done, comes out into the streets to take part in a most passionate ritual in honour of cricket. The town is gay with bunting; after sunset the ancient Castle in its murmurous gardens is turned into some fairy creation by a hundred dancing coloured lights. Men and women, lads and girls, walk the "High" in fancy costume; it is, in fact, all a carnival for cricket. Of course Tonbridge is more than an historical cradle of the game. Among its industries is the manufacture of cricket balls. Thus it is that when Woolley

THE GAME IN KENT

hits one into the middle of next week, losing it for ever, the crowd can cheer with ample inducement, for the glory of Kent cricket and for the prosperity of home trade—much as the audience in Mr Arnold Bennett's Five Towns music-hall cheered the comedian who smashed crockery on a large scale. But the glory of Kent cricket for its own sake comes first. And what cricket the Kent crowds invariably do get from their county elevens!

Kent more than any other team in the country has for years past given us cricket at its best. And this has been got by the wonderful knack a Kent side possesses of doing justice at one and the same time to both the spectacular and the combative appeals of the game. A difficult job is it for a cricketer to attend at once to the demands of cricket as a match-winning affair and to cricket as a spectacle, especially if he is a master batsman. The great artist in every pursuit of life is an egoist who must needs indulge his own exquisite zest for his own exquisite accomplishment to a point which takes him far from solicitude for the work of others. In cricket, the artist-batsman falls in love utterly with square cuts and leg glances for their own wonderful sake, and meanwhile the clock goes round and a draw looms on the score board. So much time is necessary for a complete exhibition of a Ranji's or a Fry's art. A few years ago the Sussex masters gave us the greatest spectacular cricket imaginable; every match was one long processional sweep to a mammoth total. Yet the game so played did not please; too many matches were unfinished. As much as we love the pageantry of cricket do we love the " wigs on the green," the sheer conflict.

On the other hand, the teams in the North of England, playing on wickets rather more after the bowler's heart than the wickets in the South, have perhaps gone to the other extreme and insisted overmuch on the tug-of-war aspect of cricket. A philosophy of collectivism has been potent in the building of Northern elevens; "The game is more than the player of the game" has served as the working principle. Short shrift here for the over-indulgent individualist, the artist too fond of a cultivation of the Fine Shades! Too many Lancashire, Nottinghamshire, and Yorkshire elevens have overdone the collectivist philosophy, turning out just "utility" teams, mechanically efficient.

Kent cricketers usually manage to strike the right balance; they win matches, yet they win them entrancingly. Where has cricket found artists more fascinating than Kenneth Hutchings, the Rev. W. Rashleigh, Mason, Dillon, Woolley, Blythe, D. W. Carr, Burnup, Blaker, A. P. Day, and Frank Marchant? And where match-winners of such calibre? I do not know which factor contributes most to the fashioning of Kent cricketers in this sunny way. Is it the southern temperament? Is it the setting in which Kent grounds stand, deep in the heart of gracious landscapes? Who could be sullen with grass about so fresh and green, and old nodding trees? And what cricketer can own a lightsome

THE GAME IN KENT

heart in the murk of Bramall Lane? Yet it is possible some definitely practical usage has a share in cultivating the brightness of Kent cricket. There are the "nurseries," for instance, which take young professionals well in time and coach them to play the game as attractively as any amateur from a public school. Why the idea of the Kentish nursery has not caught on all over the North of England is inexplicable. The crowds will flock to a team which can play the game in the Kentish way, with grace and gusto. But in the North of England we have mere "ground staffs," with their stark atmosphere of utility and those appalling nets wherein the hearts of scores of young bowlers have been broken to make a club member's half-holiday.

This Lancashire and Kent match was one of the very best, a game played in the ideal setting, between two keen, clever, and sportsmanlike sides, on a wicket which gave both batsman and bowler a chance, with a splendid crowd which though it wanted Kent to win yet cheered the victors most generously at the finish. All honour to Dean and Ernest Tyldesley. Thirty-eight runs were needed for a Lancashire victory when Dean came in. The bowlers had swept all before them; the Kent fielding, too, was simply magnificent. And there remained only Cook to bat had Dean failed at this point. Everyone of us hung on to Dean's slightest movement at the crease—Ernest Tyldesley we trusted implicitly. Yet it was actually Dean that put an end to our agony. He smote Woolley for a grand six over the rails, and in the same over made three other fine hits, scoring in all 18 from the great Woolley at a moment when runs were priceless. What moral courage must have gone to the smiting of that six. Imagine it for yourself. You are your side's last line of defence: victory is within reach. A great slow bowler who you may depend knows what he is doing tosses you one up in the air. Heaven help you! How can you trust that seemingly innocent ball? Would a Woolley bowl a half volley in that hour of crisis? Dare you go for it? If you do and you fail, get stumped or caught in the long field, will you not be forever reproached by your side for sheer recklessness? Yet here is the ball coming, ever so "hittable," so it would seem. You must waste no time, you must jump to it resolutely, the bat must flash down straight like lightning—there is always a margin of error in such a stroke from a spinning slow ball, a moment when you fling your bat at the flight and trust to the gods. All these thoughts must have gone through Dean's mind in one palpitating second, and he decided to go for it. If ever one good, honest clout won a match it was this. Dean's innings was in every way a little masterpiece; it combined skill and cool grit. And so, of course, was Ernest Tyldesley's.

CHAPTER VI

"W. G."

IN the Memorial Biography of W. G. Grace are sung the praises of the greatest of all cricketers. Many famous men do homage to the Grand Old Man's mastery—some of those who played the game with him in his prime; some of them cricketers of the present day who, babes in swaddling clothes at the time he was hitting his mightiest centuries, yet found him still a power in the land when they themselves came to ripeness. And the testimony is not only from masters of " W. G.'s " own craft; an Anglican Canon vies with a Peer of the Realm in polishing the lustre of his name. Page after page the deep-chested unison goes, telling over again his processional motion from triumph to triumph. " Had Grace been born in Ancient Greece," the book concludes, in the Bishop of Hereford's words, " the Iliad would have been different. Had he lived in the Middle Ages he would have been a Crusader, and would now have been lying with his legs crossed in some ancient abbey. As he was born when the world was older, he was the best-known of all Englishmen and king of cricket."

Grace was certainly the most famous man of his day, if fame consists in being talked about by the largest number of perfect strangers. He was institutional; people regarded him and discussed him just as they regarded and discussed Mr Gladstone and the National Debt. It did not matter at all whether or not you yourself were interested in cricket, you came under a social obligation to say something about him at dinner. You might even have been a professor of economics, with marginal utility the main thing on your mind, yet it was up to you to begin the conversation by asking how many " W. G." had made that day. Grace was so famous indeed, that among public men of his period he was the most readily recognised of them all by the man in the street, no matter in what part of the country he might travel. People actually crossed the high seas to witness a century by Grace. A newspaper of the day notes that as soon as the merest whisper of an innings by Grace at Lord's was breathed in the City " all the Clubs emptied and a stream of cabs dashed towards St. John's Wood." There was no end at all to his renown. Children at school put down his name in all seriousness amongst the seven wonders of the world, omitting, no doubt, the Hanging Gardens of Babylon; he was in *Punch* every week; the Royal Family was concerned about him from time to time. He was the solitary subject of thought with the great bowlers of the day; they even sat up late at night, getting rather cross about him and exchanging points of strategy. Tom Emmett used to have bad dreams about him; the story goes that the Yorkshireman once brought on a violent nightmare by falling asleep

"W. G."

just as he was forming a mental picture of the consequences to him should " W. G." some day hit back a slow ball straight. There was no talk about " brightening " cricket in Grace's time. The crowds followed him everywhere. And on those rare occasions when he failed! People rubbed their eyes; it was as though something had gone awry with the proper order and fitness of things. The bowler, no matter how seasoned a veteran he might be, would throw his cap into the air like a schoolboy. Then he would remember that there was another innings tomorrow, and think better of it, especially after that bodeful glance from glistening eyes as the Old Man passed the wicket on his way back to the pavilion. Grace's mastery was so complete, indeed, that in 1871 it was proposed that the rules of cricket be altered that bowlers might the better cope with him. " I puts the ball where I likes," was the comment of J. C. Shaw, a master of his craft, " but that beggar, he puts it where *he* likes."

" W. G.'s " record in first-class cricket begins with seven completed innings in 1865, his age then being 17. It continues, without the break of a single summer, until 1908. In that time he scored 54,896 runs in 1388 innings, average 39.55. He also captured 2864 wickets at 17.97 each. These figures boggle the imagination, but they do not reveal the fundamental point of his greatness. For one thing, Grace, for the best part of his career, played on wickets the like of which are not known in these days of marl and the heavy roller. More important still is this fact; it is the great fact of Grace's fame. He invented modern batting. It is not sufficiently borne in mind even by " W. G.'s " most ardent worshippers that at the time he took to cricket, overarm bowling had been the fashion for only some thirty years. And the amount of cricket played in a summer in that age was so small that those thirty seasons could nowadays be rolled into a mere half-dozen. Grace thus came upon a batting technique developed out of an obsolete attack, and at once changed it into the fully orchestrated thing it is to-day. He took the best points of Fuller Pilch's forward method and combined them with a back-play all his own. He demonstrated to a rather scandalised cricket field that a straight ball, dead on the wicket, could be driven; he taught the cut; he managed the then new offbreak, even as Hobbs manages it to-day, by forcing it off his pads to the on-side. He invented the difficult science of placing the ball, and out of this arose the mobile field instead of the fixed one. He invented footwork. Cricketers before his coming played forward well enough, but they rarely combined it with back play. Grace brought his legs into action as a defensive factor, only not in the decadent modern manner. He did not jump in front of the wicket, leaving the ball alone, with a divine trust in the umpire and the l.b.w. rule; no batsman left fewer balls alone than Grace, as Lord Harris points out in this biography. But Grace made the left pad go out alongside the bat in forward play, and the right leg go back with it in back play, so closely keeping the

"W. G."

two together in both movements that it was almost impossible for the ball to get past the combination. The best thing ever said about Grace's batting is written down, with a dash of high poetry, in Ranjitsinhji's "Jubilee Book of Cricket": "He turned the single-stringed instrument into the many-chorded lyre."

That "W. G." worked his way each summer to a high place in the bowling averages is the best indication possible of his zeal for cricket. Really, he was not a bowler by nature: his action was clumsy, without the free swing of the man born to the work. There can be little doubt that he took to bowling simply because he could not bear for a solitary moment to be out of the picture. He could not always be getting runs; the other side *had* to bat sooner or later. Very well, then; he was the man to get them out. A. G. Steel has left us the classic description of "W. G." in action as a bowler—"... an enormous man rushing up to the wickets with both elbows out, a great black beard blowing on both sides of him, a huge yellow cap on top of a dark, swarthy face." He was easily the most spectacular man that ever played a game. He was shaggy and ponderous, with muscular arms, capacious hands, and immense feet. He ambled about the field rather than walked, and as the players gathered together for conversation at the fall of a wicket his giant dimensions overtopped them all, making everybody else seem mere children. He was the Dr Johnson of cricket—as full of his subject, as kindly and as irascible, and just as dogmatic in his dispensations of authority. It has been well said of him that on the field he took a second place to none, not even to the umpire. Even from his seat in the pavilion where, according to all the rules and procedure of cricket he was "out of play," he must needs dominate the scene. During a Surrey and Gloucestershire match at the Oval a favourite of " W. G.'s " was given out. Up rose the Old Man from the pavilion balcony and thundered over the ground: " Shan't have it; can't have it; and I won't have it." Though he be fielding at deep square leg he would appeal vociferously for " l.b.w.", no matter how ill-placed such a position for making any sort of judgment on the point. C. I. Thornton tells a good story neatly quizzing this particular excess of zeal. " W. G." was fielding at right angles to the wicket, and Roberts, the Gloucestershire fast bowler, hit a batsman plumb on the pad. At the end of the over " W. G." said, " Why didn't you appeal for that l.b.w. ?" "Well, sir," the bowler replied, " the truth is I was waiting for you to." On another occasion a batsman disputed an l.b.w. decision on an appeal made by Grace, off his own bowling. The champion simply raised his head and thundered: " Pavilion, you." The batsman retired instantly.

But when all has been said about " W. G.'s " skill as a cricketer, we are far enough from the secret of his power over countless thousands of his countrymen. The truth is that they found in him something closer to the common heart than immense science and

"W. G."

prodigious energy. With the average man it was not Grace's hundreds alone that compelled devotion, not Grace's bowling and his fielding; it was just the Grand Old Man's zest, his perfectly English zest, for a game. No man ever flung himself into a game more passionately than "W. G." With what scorn he would have met Mr Shaw's taunt that the Englishman turns his games into hard work. Grace, who knew cricket so intimately, whose innermost nature responded swiftly to every demand made upon it by cricket, understood well that a great national game is not a mere plaything for indolent men, but a perpetual test and challenge, to which he might answer worthily only by giving up at once and gladly all that was in him of patience, courage, watchfulness, endurance and largeness of heart. There is no finer praise to be offered to cricket than that for the complete expression of its genius, through W. G. Grace, all these attributes of character were sternly called for. And there can be no better tribute to the Grand Old Man's memory than this: that he was not found wanting in the test.

CHAPTER VII

LORD'S IN WET WEATHER

(*June* 1920)

For want of something better to do during these last two incredibly wet days at Lord's, I have been trying to understand why that place so forcibly recalls Charles Dickens's " Bleak House." It is not merely that the rain has turned the place into another Chesney Wold : that the view from the pavilion window as I write is alternately a lead-coloured view and a view in Indian ink ; that the heavy drops fall, drip, drip, drip, upon the pavilion terrace, which might be named the Ghosts' Walk, since the shades of so many great cricketers of other days make it murmurous. No, not simply these external and quite accidental weather effects are responsible for the mind's jumping back to Dickens's novel. Lord's is capable of reminding you of Sir Leicester Dedlock and Chesney Wold in fine weather as well as in wet, so inflexibly aristocratic is the place, so proud of the ceremonies, so insistent on blue blood.

Unless one happens to be definitely of Lord's, and a member of the mighty M.C.C., one is outside the pale here. You are inexorably kept at a distance. The place is a mass of signboards, teaching you your manners and position in life. Like Sir Leicester Dedlock all over, Lord's is as old as the hills, and, so it would appear, infinitely more respectable. The place, indeed, carries a general air of believing that the world might get on without hills, but would be done up without the M.C.C. Since Nature made the grass which grows there, Lord's would, no doubt, admit with Sir Leicester, that, on the whole, Nature is a good idea, but an idea just a little low when not enclosed with a fence. There is even to this day at Lord's a kind of fence which separates amateurs from professionals. A man from the unfashionable North, carrying with him a suggestion of real industry, feels that Lord's is all the time eyeing him curiously from a safe point of vantage, and mentally putting him down as a possible Wat Tyler, or, at the most generous estimate, an Ironfounder.

It is hard to imagine there is any place in the world where class distinctions are so firmly stressed as at Lord's. During a University match this is more apparent than ever. That is why possibly no painter in the school of Frith has given us a canvas depicting Lord's on a fine summer's day during the occasion of a 'Varsity match. The picture would certainly give scope for something of the multitudinous panorama in Frith's too much abused " Derby Day," but it would be bound to miss the broad universal appeal of the racing picture. Human nature on a large scale could hardly be got into a view of Lord's—only one aspect of it, well bred and exclusive. A race meeting, on the other hand, annihilates class distinctions.

A CRICKETER'S BOOK

What would happen to a man in corduroys at Lord's (supposing for the sake of argument such a phenomenon possible)—what would happen to him if he smote a Viscount on the back in the throes of some enthusiasm for a leg hit? Yet at a race meeting such events have been known to happen, to nobody's consternation. One touch of Epsom with the favourite in fourth at 6 to 4 on makes the whole world kin. Still, after all, these fine aristocratic ways at Lord's do not really annoy. Possibly an American visitor would find them objectionable. That is because he would not regard them, as they are regarded by the average outsider, who pays his couple of shillings at Lord's, as just a pretty decoration on the main structure of affairs. Lord's will not allow the man in the street to come right into the swim, but they can't keep him right out. I saw a few working men this morning at the ground gates waiting for the rain to stop. They variously wore light and dark blue colours. How each man decided whether Oxford or Cambridge should be the vent for the expression of his inveterate partisanship I could not say. His interest in both elevens might well have been merely academic. But it was not so—these same working men were rather hot with argument about the respective qualities of Bettington, Marriott, Hedges and Partridge. Obviously the game is more than the player of the game, in Kipling's words, even at Lord's, and common human nature will creep in. The terrible rain to-day could not keep it quite out.

CHAPTER VIII

TOM RICHARDSON

ON June 26, 1902, Old Trafford was a place of Ethiopic heat, and the crowd that sat there in an airless world saw J. T. Tyldesley flog the Surrey bowlers all over the field. Richardson attacked from the Stretford end, and at every over's finish he wiped the sweat from his brow and felt his heart beating hammer strokes. Richardson had all his fieldsmen on the off side, save one, who " looked out " at mid on. And once (and once only) he bowled a long hop to Tyldesley, who swung on his heels and hooked the ball far into the on field. The Surrey fieldsman at mid wicket saw something pass him, and with his eye helplessly followed the direction of the hit. " One boundary more or less don't count on a day like this," it was possible to imagine the sweltering fellow telling himself, " Besides, Johnny's plainly going to get 'em anyhow." The ball slackened pace on the boundary's edge. Would it just roll home ? The crowd tried to cheer it to the edge of the field. Then one was aware of heavy thuds on the earth. Some Surrey man, after all, had been fool enough to think a desperate spurt and a boundary saved worth while, blistering sun despite. Who on earth was the stout but misguided sportsman ?

Heaven be praised, it was Richardson himself. He had bowled the ball; he had been bowling balls, and his fastest, for nearly two hours. His labours in the sun had made ill those who sat watching him. And here he was, pounding along the outfield, after a hit from his own bowling. The writer sat on the " popular " side, under the score-board, as the ball got home a foot in advance of Richardson. The impetus of his run swept him over the edge of the grass, and to stop himself he put out his arms and grasped the iron rail. He laughed—the handsomest laugh in the world—and said " Thank you " to somebody who threw the ball back to him. His face was wet, his breath scant. He was the picture of honest toil. With the ball in his hands again he trotted back to the wicket and once more went through the travail of bowling at J. T. Tyldesley on a pitiless summer's day.

This was Tom Richardson all over—the cricketer whose heart was so big that even his large body hardly contained its heroic energy. And this hot June morning the crowd mused about a day that had dragged out an intolerable length six years earlier—in 1896—on which England had struggled bitterly with Australia at Old Trafford, and Tom Richardson had touched as sublime a heroism as ever cricketer knew. This Manchester Test match of July, 1896, seems now to have been fought on so vast a scale that it might well be thought none but giants could have sustained the burden of it. Yet when Richardson's part in it is retold he was a very

TOM RICHARDSON

colossus that made pigmies of the others—made even Ranji a pigmy, despite that he played the innings of his life.

Australia batted first and scored 412. England—with Grace, Ranji, Stoddart, Abel, Jackson, J. T. Brown, MacLaren, Lilley, and Briggs to look to for runs—were all out for 231, and the Australian captain sent us in again. And once more the English cracks were reduced to littleness—all save Ranji, who, in Giffen's term, " conjured " an innings of 154 not out, out of the total of 305. Australia needed 125 for victory—a mere song on the wicket. Old Trafford gave itself up to the doldrums as soon as Iredale and Trott had comfortably made a score or so without loss. Then it was that Richardson's face was seen to be grim—his customary happy smile gone. In Australia's first innings he had bowled 68 overs for seven wickets and 168 runs. Yet he was here again, bowling like a man just born to immortal energy. And four Australian wickets were down for 45 in an hour. If only England had given the Australians a few more runs, the crowd wished out of its heart—if only Richardson could keep up his pace for another hour. But, of course, no man could expect him to bowl in this superhuman vein for long. . . . Thus did the crowd sigh and regret. But Richardson's spirit *did* go on burning a dazzling flame. The afternoon moved slowly to the sunset—every hour an eternity. And Richardson *did* bowl and bowl and bowl, and his fury diminished not a jot. Other English bowlers faltered, but not

Richardson. The fifth Australian wicket fell at 79, the sixth at 95, the seventh at 100. The Australians now wanted 25, with only three wickets in keeping, McKibbin and Jones—two rabbits—amongst them. "Is it possible?" whispered the crowd. "Can it be? Can we win . . . after all? . . ." Why, look at Richardson and see: England must win. This man is going to suffer no frustration. He has bowled for two hours and a half, without a pause. He has bowled till Nature has pricked him with protesting pains in every nerve, in every muscle of his great frame. He has bowled till Nature can no longer make him aware that she is abused outrageously, for now he is a man in a trance, the body of him numbed and moving automatically to the only suggestion his consciousness can respond to—" England must win, must win, must win." . . . With nine runs still to be got by Australia, Kelly gave a chance to Lilley at the wicket and Lilley let the ball drop to the earth. The heart of Richardson might have burst at this, but it did not. To the end he strove and suffered.

Australia won by three wickets, and the players ran from the field—all of them save Richardson. He stood at the bowling crease, dazed. *Could* the match have been lost? his spirit protested. Could it be that the gods had looked on and permitted so much painful striving to go by unrewarded? His body still shook from the violent motion. He stood there like some fine animal baffled at the uselessness of great strength and effort in this world. . . . A companion

TOM RICHARDSON

led him to the pavilion, and there he fell wearily to a seat. That afternoon Richardson had laboured for three mortal hours without surcease. In the match he bowled 110 overs and three balls, for 13 wickets and 244 runs. He never bowled again in a Test match at Manchester.

This man Richardson was the greatest cricketer that ever took to fast bowling. Lockwood had nicer technical shades than Richardson—a guile which was alien to the honest heart of Richardson. But Lockwood had not a great spirit. He was a bowler at the mercy of a mood; an artist with an artist's capriciousness. Richardson bowled from a natural impulse to bowl, and whether he bowled well or ill that impulse was always strong. His action moved one like music because it was so rhythmical. He ran to the wicket a long distance, and at the bowling crease his terminating leap made you catch breath. His breakback most cricketers of his day counted among the seven wonders of the game. He could pitch a ball outside the wicket on the hardest turf and hit the leg stump. The break was, of course, an action break; at the moment of " release " his fingers swept across the ball and the body was flung towards the left. And his length was as true as Attewell's own. But who is going to talk of Richardson's art in terms of the " filthily technical," as Mr Kipling would call it ? His bowling was wonderful because into it went the very life-force of the man—the triumphant energy that made him in his hey-day seem one of Nature's announcements of the joy of life. It was sad to see

Richardson grow old, to see the fires in him burn low. Cricketers like Richardson would not know old age in the "Never Never Land" of our desires. Every springtime ought to find them newborn, like the green world they live in.

CHAPTER IX

TWO WONDERFUL BOYS

HAS the game ever known two schoolboys who announced all-round genius more eloquently than A. G. Steel and J. N. Crawford? Some of the old men who sit in the pavilion, and as they look over the field, now and then seem to be looking again into a remote past indeed—some of these may be able to name a boy they knew better at all the points of the game than Steel and Crawford; but the writer has not heard of him. Grace, of course, was top of the English averages at the age of 16, but he never bowled in the great bowler's way. C. L. Townsend, when he was 17, bowled beautifully for Gloucestershire, but his batting then had no uncommon distinction. F. S. Jackson did not develop into a great batsman till his third year at Cambridge. C. T. Studd was 22 when he scored 1,000 runs and took 100 wickets in a season. But Crawford achieved the " double event " at the age of 19, and Steel was top of the English bowling averages at 19—his record 164 wickets at 9 runs each—and a year later he was fourth in the English batting averages, above Scotton, Lucas, Ulyett, I. D. Walker, and A. J. Webbe.

The great point about these boys is that while still at school both might well have played for England.

Crawford led the bowling averages for the country in 1904, with yet a year to serve at Repton, and he played for England in South Africa in the winter following his last summer at school. Steel did not win international honours till he was 22, but that was because not till 1880 did an authentic Test match between England and Australia happen in this country. We have the authority of W. J. Ford for believing that Steel was never better as a bowler than during his last year at Marlborough.

Crawford as a boy bowled medium pace and Steel slow to slow medium. There, as far as the bowling of the two boys goes, similarity ends. Steel had a most ample bag of tricks, including both the off and the leg breaks. Crawford never, to the writer's knowledge, broke from leg. He relied on a rare off-break and pace variations. As batsmen the two boys were fashioned in the same mould, or perhaps it would be better to say, out of the same stuff. Each was a masterful maker of runs, eager to take the offensive. Steel did not have Crawford's lovely stance at the wicket; he crouched a little, and Mr R. H. Lyttelton has put down this inelegance to Steel's lack of really good eyesight. Crawford also lacked a naturally good vision, but he had the sense to play cricket in glasses.

But better, perhaps, if we now look at these prodigies one at a time. Steel's first dose of first-class cricket came to him in 1878, as a member of the greatest of all Cambridge XI.'s, which contained these cricketers: A. P. Lucas, A. Lyttelton, E.

TWO WONDERFUL BOYS

Lyttelton, H. Whitfield, D. Q. Steel, L. K. Jarvis, A. G. Steel, F. W. Kingston, Ivo Bligh, P. H. Morton, and A. F. J. Ford. This team played eight matches, including one against an Australian XI., and won them all. Steel headed the batting averages of this superb XI., his innings worth 87 each, and took 75 wickets at an average of 7. In the same summer of 1878 Steel, a youth of 19, bowled for Lancashire against Yorkshire and helped himself to 14 wickets for 112 runs. The story got about that Tom Emmett, when he heard Steel was playing for Lancashire in that match, said to his companions, " Let's go home, lads; Steel's playing, and Yorkshire's beat ! "

One does not often hear mentioned the most wonderful point of all about Steel's cricket. This, surely, is that he could as a boy attain to mastery in just that kind of bowling which needs to be deployed craftily, with a profound insight into the niceties of batsmanship. A slow left-handed bowler may do well as a boy—as Rhodes did—and cause no out-of-way problem, for the reason that the left-handed bowler starts with an advantage given to him by nature over the right-handed batsman. His line of flight comes into the batsman awkwardly, and the " break away " is in strong contrast with the line of flight. The slow right-handed bowler starts with no such natural advantage; his line of flight is pretty direct to a right-handed batsman. Most of the great slow bowlers have been left-handers—Briggs, Blythe, Peel. Slow or even slow medium right-hand bowlers usually require the strategy that is only got from long service in the game, before they cause great trouble. But young Steel tossed his slows along to some of the greatest batsmen that ever lived, and never was it easy for them to get him on the half volley, despite that, with youth's own audacity, he over-pitched rather than under-pitched. There was a famous occasion at Old Trafford when he " teased " Shrewsbury to the stage of making Shrewsbury look undignified. He tossed the ball higher and higher into the air, dropping it in the crease almost. Yet Shrewsbury regarded every delivery as though the ball had an imp of mischief inside, and declined to move his bat unwarily. Steel was the perfect example of the " tricky " bowler, getting his men out by bluff as much as by the technical quality of his bowling. Can ever a boy have played the game with an older head than Steel's on his shoulders ?

Steel's batting in his prime was masterful. His averages hardly tell how great he was as a runmaker. He got himself out almost as often as the bowlers. His confidence was genius's own : he seemed to assume as a matter of course superiority over the best bowler. He did not content himself, as your modern batsman does, with waiting for loose balls. In his day loose balls were not as prodigally sent along as they are to-day. Steel, in form, hit the bowling when it was on the wicket, and when it was not on the wicket he went after it, and hit it as soon as he found it. The innings he played at Lord's in 1884 for England against the Australians is to this

TWO WONDERFUL BOYS

day talked over with some ecstasy by the old 'uns who saw it. The bowlers were Spofforth, Boyle, Palmer, and Giffen, and they might well have been blinded by the white light that Steel spread about him as he hit his flashing boundaries. W. G. Grace once said of Steel that he should never forget the "cheeky" way Steel laid about the Australian bowlers. He had no qualms about jumping out of his ground to Spofforth's notorious slow ball and banging it to the edge of the field. Not that he was a reckless hitter; the pace of his batsmanship was swift because he was master of every stroke and quick and light on his feet.

J. N. Crawford, it may seem, has no bright prospect in a comparison with Steel. Yet the writer can hardly believe that even Steel was a better batsman than Crawford at his best. It may be said Steel made runs brilliantly against greater bowlers than ever Crawford had to face, but Crawford has the right of answering that that was no fault of his. In form, he made the bowlers he *had* to tackle look so helpless that they might easily have been twice as good and still not escaped punishment. Perhaps the writer, in suggesting that Crawford was as good as Steel as a batsman, is still dazed by the splendour of an innings of Crawford's he saw played against the Australian Imperial Forces XI. of 1919, at the Oval. Gregory was in that Australian side, and a more formidable bowler then than he was last summer, save at Trent Bridge in the first Test match. At the Oval in 1919 on the occasion one has in mind Gregory bowled a tremendous pace and repeatedly broke back. He " went through " four Surrey batsmen, including Hobbs, for a score or so of runs. C. T. A. Wilkinson stopped him bravely for a while, and then Crawford came in and flogged the fast bowler as surely fast bowler was never flogged before. The innings was incredibly brilliant. Gregory was driven straight as though he were bowling underhand lobs. His short " bumpers " were most dramatically hooked to the boundary. The last Surrey wicket that afternoon scored 80 runs, and Crawford made 78 of them in fifty minutes. In all he batted for two hours and ten minutes, scored 144 not out, and hit two sixes, one five, and eighteen fours.

None but a master could have played this innings. Yet, brilliant batsman though Crawford was in this country—like Steel he had only himself to blame for many a brief innings,—Australians declare that it was in their own country that Crawford's genius as a batsman really came to the flower. Crawford's career with Surrey ended in 1909, and he went to Australia. There he played for South Australia, and his batsmanship was written down by Australian judges of cricket as the most brilliant since Trumper. Mr Warner has said Crawford was a greater batsman in Australia than he was here, and he ought to know, for it was against Mr Warner's 1911-12 team that Crawford played, at Brisbane, an innings of 110 against Rhodes, F. R. Foster, Barnes, Woolley, Hearne, and Iremonger, and batted a mere hour and a half, put even Barnes in a little way, and drove two

TWO WONDERFUL BOYS

sixes and fifteen boundaries. Crawford probably had not as many strokes as Steel, but his driving, especially his straight driving, can hardly have been second in combined power and precision to the driving of any orthodox batsman in the records of cricket. His style had, with all the fury of his hitting, an exquisite forward poise; his power came from a driving mechanism that worked in perfect time, not from excessive muscular effort. The writer can speak from experience of Crawford's driving. He played against him when Crawford was at Repton, and even then, though a frail slip of a boy, Crawford put a force into his hitting that made the field lively indeed. We took a sort of pity on Crawford that day, when he first came in to bat; he looked so little like a cricketer, what with his slender body and his spectacles. And for a while we bowled " nice ones " to him. Then we got tired of charity and unloosed our heaviest batteries. And the faster we bowled the more young Crawford smote us. There was genius in his every movement at the wicket.

Crawford probably cannot stand discussion as a bowler in the same breath that discusses Steel's bowling, but that is only because Steel was a bowler in a thousand. Crawford certainly stood in the front rank of the bowlers of 1904-9, and certain it is that we have no bowler to-day as good as Crawford at his best. His wonderful break-back he could make bite even on the pluperfect Australian wickets. This amazing spin he got by holding the ball with the second finger, as well as the first, giving " purchase " to the ball. With this break went a beautiful length —on his best days. His bowling in the Test matches in Australia in 1907-8 was after the grand manner. Despite the hard wickets, the heat, and the fact that he was on a losing side, he took 30 wickets at 24.70 each—this against batsmen of the Trumper, Hill, Noble, Duff calibre, and in their own land too. Barnes, when he was in his greatest Australian form during the winter of 1911-12, had to pay 22.88 each for his 34 wickets, and he had stronger support than Crawford. Few English bowlers have been put to the test of sterner Australian bats than faced Crawford in 1907-8, when he had barely reached manhood; few have had to toil on grounds more heartbreaking than those on which this wonderful boy toiled. And few, indeed, have come through the ordeal as handsomely as Crawford.

The old men on the pavilion are rightly proud of the cricketers who made history "in their day." For good reason, too, may they be jealous of the old masters' honours. But they will surely be magnanimous when they consider the genius of young Crawford, and not think some slight comparison of him with the magnificent A. G. Steel intolerably odious.

CHAPTER X

THE RETURN OF CRICKET
(Any April)

AT this time of the year the re-birth of cricket is being observed the country over with all appropriate rites. Men are taking up their old boots and knocking last September's turf out of the spikes, now sweet brown powder, fragrant to the memory. They are busy whitening these same old boots again—no true cricketer ever buys a new pair until he is compelled—with a small sponge and a tin of blanco, taking tremendous pains to go over the buckskin without smearing the soles. The bat comes from the shelf; it is fondled lovingly, and that slightly splintered edge is regarded concernedly. It was done in getting a fast one from Smith to the on side. Couldn't have been a good shot, now we come to think of it! One ought really to get the ball in the middle of the bat. Still, it was a good enough shot for a country-house game, and all boundaries look alike on the score card.

The groundsman is out already tending his pitch, his eye as keen for the fine shades as any Whistler over a nocturne. Hear him startle that barbarian fellow who is actually crossing the ground on a bicycle, and the turf wet! He puts two fingers over his nether lip and makes a noise whose piercing quality can be heard a mile away. Fellow on bicycle ignominiously swerves to the path, trying to look as if he had already been going in that direction anyway. The men are fixing the nets at the far corner of the enclosure, and somebody is already waking the echoes of the pavilion as he walks along the platform of wooden laths. What a strange charm there is in the hollow echoes of a cricket pavilion! And what a ritual lies in the opening of a cricket pavilion after a winter of solitude and quiet! It must, of course, be a place devoted wholly to cricket, where no alien footballers come in midwinter to disturb its silences. The lock is stiff, and rightly so, for sacrilege would be committed by an abrupt disturbance of this murmurous sanctuary. Inside, you get the familiar odour which might be supposed to come from the essence of a hundred bygone mellow days. On the forms are those dirty grey pads, with the buckle off the right-legged one. The very deuce to get it on, when you are next man in all of a sudden and you can see, from the shady interior, through the square, glassless window, the other man coming from the wicket out of the warm sunshine. And from the hooks on the wall there is hanging that very shirt, sleeves hopelessly inside out, which you left last backend, and there it has been all through the gloom and chill of winter. It is a reminder that one often plays the game for the last time at the end of a summer without knowing it is the last time. Of course that

THE RETURN OF CRICKET

way of taking leave of the greatest of games for ever so many long, dreary months is all wrong. A good cricketer ought to finish a season consciously performing a valedictory ceremony. He should feel the pathos of the farewell as the September sun falls lower and lower in the sky, and the shadows lengthen on the calm grass. The declining moments should exude bitter-sweet pain. The grey early autumn mists rising round the quiet ground should strike one as the harbinger of the end, and with the last over the pageant of the dead season should pass rather sadly before the mind's eye. How exquisite, if one felt all this, would be the solemnity of the final drawing of stumps and the homeward walk to the pavilion. One would then murmur to oneself, drawing out to the full the fine sentimentality of the scene and the occasion, HÆC OLIM MEMINISSE JUVABIT!

Happy is it that one is in no danger of missing a jot of the sense of the event when one begins a new season. Let it be a balmy April day, and how can we fail to catch the joy that comes as we feel the air filling out our flannels, making us luxuriously loose at the neck, and passing over the body with a gentle caress? Good Lord, we must ask ourselves, what lives we do lead in the winter! How absurd now seems the best Wilton overcoat in the world, and the softest of silk scarves! This is the sweet o' the year.

The occasion has its pains and penalties, none the less. A batsman sends his willow out like a flail, and hits quite a yard over a miserable half-volley.

Heaven help me, he might well ask himself, why do they make bats so impossibly heavy? How, in the name of justice, do they expect a mere mortal to hit a ball so outrageously small? Yet once upon a time, the distraught man tells himself, he was known to hit it, aye, even to the boundary. Will he ever accomplish the feat again? So, too, does the bowler have his moments of misgiving, as he strains his creaking joints into activity after the winter's period of coma. The problem with him is to get the ball even half-way down the pitch, and he is thinking of writing an indignant letter to the papers asking the M.C.C. to go in for a projectile whose specific gravity it might conceivably be within human power to control with dignity.

Then comes that morning after the first practice. What cricketer does not know it? You wake up feeling there is an uncommonly large amount of you in bed, all ribs. It is as though somebody had gone over you in the night with a hard brick. At breakfast an occasion rises for laughter. You are not equal to it. Your state is, in Mr Pecksniff's phrase, "chronic." Yet, how marked off from the rest of mankind you feel when you take your seat in the tramcar. You have been through a rigorous spring cleaning. You are now a being definitely of thew and sinew. The man next you is in the way of being a worm. For you are full of fresh air and rich red blood. He is just a colloid, in an overcoat, and probably he is asthmatical. How can you be expected to pity him, feeling as you do, as hard as nails?

THE RETURN OF CRICKET

There is the season before you, too, and yesterday's misgiving are gone. You are determined to leave last season's average a long way behind. If only you can resist the ball on the " off " that goes away . . .

Yes, it is indeed the sweet o' the year for cricketers —the world just green fresh grass and sunshine, and jolly companions in white.

CHAPTER XI

ON TAKING A GAME TOO SERIOUSLY

(June 1921)

At the Oval last Tuesday morning a little event happened upon which might be hung a tale of some use to cricketers at the moment. A great innings was in the making by J. N. Crawford, who put a confident face to these dreadful Australians and touched his batsmanship with the imperial purple. And then, just as this little innings promised greatness, J. N. Crawford was most unfortunately run out by Ducat, whereat the crowd made most mournful noises in protest. Even in the pavilion, a place from which it was impossible to pass intelligent judgment on the umpire's decision—even there disgruntled moans went up to the sky. But Crawford himself, as he returned to the pavilion, his masterpiece shattered, carried himself pleasantly. "Hard luck," said somebody in the pavilion to Crawford, who simply smiled and responded " Never mind." Here is our moral: the game stands in some need to-day of men who can smile and say " Never mind." We are taking our cricket much too seriously: whoever sees a cricketer with a happy air about him in these times ? It is not simply that we are in the doldrums through

ON TAKING A GAME TOO SERIOUSLY

the defeats against the Australians. It is a gloomy spirit that has come into the game wholesale, one that has, indeed, afflicted the Australian game not less than ours. Could a man have imagined the other Monday afternoon at Lord's that the Australians were winning the second Test match? The faces of all of them were set in lines of sheer pain. One recalled the story about the man who was looking upon the Winged Victory of Samothrace for the first time. He asked the name of it. "Why," said his companion, "that is the famous Victory statue." "Well," replied our innocent abroad, "if that's 'Victory' I'd like to see the other fellow!" We have not yet seen the Australians in defeat, but they take their victories harrowingly enough.

Cricket, the summer game, is becoming too much of a purely combative business for the happy spirit of it. It is assuming a hardness and a grimness better fitted for the wintry days than for June. It is, of course, good to have "the wigs on the green" at cricket, to see the men on their toes and the crowd intent and palpitating. But full homage to cricket will not come from a lust for conquest alone; it is not the best game of all if you cultivate it simply as an outlet for combative energy. Cricket is the most lovable game in the world because of its sweet amenities, its grace, and its humours. One would not, of course, wish to find slackness coming into cricket, nor to discover in our cricketers so many Laodiceans. But surely the game has once known its happy warriors? Was cricket ever so thrilling, ever so vigorously combative, in fact, as it was in the days of Hirst, Briggs, Richardson, S. M. J. Woods, J. T. Tyldesley, and Victor Trumper? If it is the spoils of war that your cricketer is after, where are better men than these nowadays to force the victory home? Yet where are there happier spirits, where cricketers truer to the loveliness, the magnanimity, and the laughing heart of the game?

> Give me the bowler whose fingers embracing me,
> Tingle and throb with the joy of the game;
> One who can laugh at a smack to the boundary,

sings E. V. Lucas. How long must he look for such a one to-day, how far? At Lord's the other week, in the Lancashire and Middlesex match, an onlooker who does not often go to a first-class game remarked on the extreme gravity of the proceedings. The two elevens, no doubt, were concentrated on the match, both " out to win." But so plainly was the occasion exclusively a combative one, so ruthlessly and completely had the uses of cricket been twisted to antagonistic issues, that one really wondered why on earth the warring factions, instead of settling differences at a game whose action is, after all, slow, and into whose element humour *will* creep—why, instead of cricket, the teams had not fought out the contention, like the gentlemen in Mark Twain, with brickbats at forty paces.

From this tendency amongst cricketers to see in the game nothing but a vent for antagonisms comes mainly the " ca' canny " policy common in first-class

ON TAKING A GAME TOO SERIOUSLY

games to-day. A man in this air sniffs ambuscades all about him; he goes the safe way, and, of course, that way routine lies. The maximum of accomplishment at the minimum of risk—here's the prevalent philosophy. "There's not one hearty poet amongst them all," says Bacchus in "The Frogs," "that's fit to risk an adventurous valiant phrase." Not quite true, this, of cricket to-day, perhaps, but all too nearly true. There are Hobbs, Macartney, Woolley, and the players at the Universities, but there is also the average professional cricketer, making a labour of the sunniest game of them all. And in the end, what shall it profit a man that he has "topped the averages," that Loamshire has kept intact its percentage? When a cricketer comes to old age, and in some brown study memory gets to work upon him, his mind will have little room in it for these issues. He will try to recapture the sense of walking on soft grass; he will recall that cricket and summer-time went together, that he lived a life then in a place which burned "as if every grass blade were a torch." The memory of good fellowship, too, will move him, and, let us hope, the memory of excellent fun. Even the umpires will come now to him in comic aspect—Dogberrys of the cricket field! These are the amenable things that cricket lives upon. Does the modern cricketer, taking him in the large, know of them? Does he often look happy at his work?

It has been shown, even in recent years, that a winning team need not scourge itself to victory. Was there ever a happier, more care-free set of cricketers than the Kent XI. that won the championship in 1906? Was there not an ample gaiety in the Lancashire side of 1904, also champions? G. K. Chesterton somewhere says that so much depends on an individual's philosophy that it ought to be considered even before one chooses one's landlady. Suppose the Selection Committee looks into a cricketer's outlook on life before asking him to play for England. Let them consider his private reading and rule out any man who has Dean Inge in any large quantity in his library. A side of Crawfords, capable of broad grins and of lusty " Damn the consequences," might conceivably stop Macdonald and Gregory. The cricketer with the best technical equipment in the world will be of scant use to us if his imagination transforms these quite human Australians into eleven men in buckram! Let the working philosophy of English cricketers, in Test matches and out of them, be, as Harry Weldon would say, " It's a game, it's a game! " And a summer game at that, with plenty of high jinks in it.

CHAPTER XII

HOBBS—AN APPRECIATION

(May 1920)

THAT the first century of the season should usually come from Hobbs is, as Mr Square in " Tom Jones " would have said, in full accordance with the eternal fitness of things. For Hobbs is indisputably our leading batsman; moreover, he is an out-and-out product of the modern game. Were a Martian to come upon us, wanting an introduction to the science of batting as we know it to-day, he need go no farther than the Oval some morning when Hobbs was at his best. And, truth to tell, Hobbs is always at his best, even if he fails to put up a big score. This is no paradox. There are cricketers who can give a glimpse of their mettle even in the very process of getting clean bowled, just as a tyro may hit a ball to the boundary time after time, yet only to convince us of his total lack of art. Whoever saw MacLaren act in any way unbecoming to a great cricketer? I always think of him to-day as I saw him once playing forward to Blythe beautifully, a majestic rhythm governing the slightest movement. He was clean bowled on the occasioin I have in mind for none, but nobody other than a giant of the game could have made a duck so immaculately. He always played cricket as some proud Roman might have played it.

Hobbs, without possessing MacLaren's eternal magnificence, can similarly convince us even on his unfruitful days. Rarely does he lose his wicket through incorrect or, rather, inartistic play. He does, of course, deviate from the conventions; that is because, like the artist he is, Hobbs cannot go on from day to day just scoring runs in the way that comes easiest to him. No artist is happy moving along the lines where resistance is least, and Hobbs is for ever seeking to widen the scope of his craft—experimenting, creating obstacles for the sheer joy of overcoming them. So does a Chopin choose to write a study for black notes only, a Chardin paint a white tablecloth against a white background! Any green boy fresh from his coach at a public school may hit a ball on the off stump past cover; Hobbs often prefers to get it round to the on with a wonderfully daring hook shot. Of course it is risky, and now and again he pays the penalty.

At the beginning of last summer (1919) an amount of gloom set in at the Oval because Hobbs failed several days in succession. Was his day over? asked the Jeremiahs. And then, just before the Lancashire match in London, Hobbs decided he had been playing a little too confidently, trying his on shots before getting the pace of the wicket. In this match he promised himself he would take no undue risk. As a result he got a century. And he would get a century every time he batted if he chose to " sit on the splice" and wait for the inevitable loose ones. Fortunately for the glory of modern cricket, Hobbs sees in the game more of art than of science. Like Peter Pan, he is ever out for "an awfully big adventure."

I have said that Hobbs in himself would provide an ample idea of the scope of modern batting technique. And I should say that the great batsman of to-day differs from the great batsman of yesterday in his fuller command over back play as an offensive factor, and his ability to combine it easefully with forward play. Men like Hobbs have worked out a method of back play such as few cricketers of the 'eighties dreamt of, though there have, of course, always been geniuses who "built wiser than they knew"— wiser, that is, than the law taught them. Such a one was Arthur Shrewsbury, whose back play was faultless, no matter how bad the wicket. But how far cricketers of yesterday were, in the lump, from realising the full scope of back play we may understand from this sentence in Grace's book on cricket:

"Whatever you do, do not get in front of the wicket when you play the ball. . . . My experience has shown me that by keeping your right foot firmly in its place and drawing back the left until the heels are almost touching, one can resort to what is called the glide stroke and place the ball to leg."

The G. O. M. was, of course, laying down a canon taught by experience of the bowling of his day. But other times other manners. Bowling is not as accurate now as it was in the Shaw and Attewell epoch, but it turns more than ever it did and is distinctly shorter. Two conclusions emerge if we consider these changes. The " classical " forward stroke was, from its very muscular action, slightly speculative; that is to say, one did not actually see the ball at the moment the bat met it. The stroke assumed that the ball on pitching would follow more or less along the line of flight. In that case the stationary right leg as a *point d'appui* for the lunge forward was a sound enough rule. If the ball turned out rather shorter than you had at first calculated, you could, as the G. O. M. instructs, play back at it simply by drawing in the left leg.

But latterly we have had scores of good bowlers (I am speaking of bowling on the average during the last dozen years) whose deliveries you could not trust to follow along the line of flight after pitching. Some of them—Vogler, Faulkner, Bosanquet, Hordern—did not even break the way their finger and wrist action indicated; they were " googly " men—bowlers of " wrong 'uns." To cope with these, the more or less speculative lunge forward was suicidal. Better to run out, if it was a case of forward play at all. Most of these men, however, bowled rather short of a length, so that if your right foot was grounded stiff just behind the popping crease you met the ball as it was turning and, what was more dangerous, still taking an upward trajectory. In 1912 the South Africans went to pieces in the Triangular Tests mainly because of immobile play on the right foot. This defect, as Mr E. H. D. Sewell once shrewdly pointed out, was probably due to the fact that in South Africa cricket is played on matting, and that a batsman tends to ground his right foot behind the edge of the matting and keep it there. Whatever the cause, fast-footedness was the South Africans' ruin against Barnes.

Batsmen like Hobbs meet the " new " bowling mainly by using the feet as batsmen never used them before. They go back right on the wicket, when they cannot jump to the pitch, thus giving the ball time to work off its spin and devil and so become more playable. They simply have to move the right leg across the wicket (to the horror of the old 'uns!) so that it may be used as a pivot on which to swing the body for the hook stroke to a break-back—the pads quite legitimately protecting the stumps. Hobbs has this stroke to perfection.

Old cricketers may argue with some force that modern batting—even that of Hobbs—is not as delightful to watch as batting was when it was three-parts forward play. The grace of forward play comes from the longer swing that can be got if you move your left leg fairly well out. But a flowing rhythmical movement is not the only way in which great batting may titillate the æsthetic emotions. If Hobbs, for instance, finds the wicket or the bowling rather against a free forward game, then he makes the main factor in his back play take the form of wrist-work. And who will deny the fascination of wrist-work? Why, the most stylish bat of the last twenty years, and that is R. H. Spooner, appealed to us less by his forward play than by wrist action used in conjunction with back-play.

With Hobbs, when he is on a bad wicket, back play is made positively dramatic. He times his strokes so beautifully that you catch your breath as you see the ball on the very wicket. Then he gives you that wonderfully quick swing round, the right leg as pivot, and you have seen the finest on-side shot of recent years! The Harrow drive through the covers is sweet, but Hobbs on the on-side is majestic. Besides, given a fast wicket, Hobbs can play the conventional forward game with the best of them. How superbly adaptable is his style we can understand from his success in this country, in South Africa, in Australia, against all conceivable sorts of bowling. The modern batsmen may have the good fortune to play on better wickets than those which fell to cricketers of yesterday, but, to be just to them, let us realise that they have bowling infinitely more diversified to tackle.*

Hobbs has mastered great bowlers in the "classical" manner, and Rhodes, Blythe, Noble, J. T. Hearne will compare with any of the bowlers of the 'eighties and 'nineties; he has also mastered the greatest of the modernists—Hordern, Schwarz, Faulkner, Barnes, Hirst, F. R. Foster, "googly" men, leg-break-cum-off-break, swerve or what you will. He learnt all the well-tried tricks of the trade from Tom Hayward, and he has added a few of his very own.

* Again, let me make it plain that I refer to bowling during the Barnes-Vogler-Foster period.

CHAPTER XIII

JOHNNY BRIGGS

He was surely born for a game, for he was a sort of little indiarubber ball of a man, and he seemingly remained in one position more than a second at a time only by strong will-power. When he walked from the pavilion at Old Trafford (under his arm that mummy of a bat of his, in the ancient binding) one had the notion that if he came down too heavily on the turf he would bounce back again into the dressing-room, through the window. Recollect how he went to the wicket. He was, one thought, like a happy boy going for a walk, or rather in quest of adventure. His eyes shone humour at you, his every movement was alive, and youthfully alive. One has known dull days and dull cricket before the advent of Briggs, but he had just to show his face and a light passed over the field, and with it a companionable warmth. He was a man into whose body the humours of summer entered day by day—sunshine, wind, and refreshing dews. No cricketer ever lived who was so much the child of nature as Briggs. This man a subtle bowler? you might well have asked, looking at his bland eyes, yet he was a very Heathen Chinee of cricket. He bowled you a left-handed ball with a quite casual motion; his arm swept over almost ingratiatingly. His run to the wicket was modest, and a little mincing. But if the turf were at all susceptible to spin, the ball he sent you had a bottle imp inside it. It might twist so viciously that a little tuft of grass was cut from the pitch; it might scuttle to the base of your stumps like a mouse; it might jump up at you and rap your knuckle abominably. Yet it was hard to be short with him, despite his deceit. He was as a child playing tricks with you. When he bowled you neck and crop there was a cocky little strut in his walk as he moved to mid-off to tell him exactly how the ball had pitched on your legs and hit your off wicket. And again it was hard to be short with him. Obviously he had bowled you in sheer fun; you simply had to join in the general laughter. He was as busy as a bee all day long. How he worried his batsman! The poor fellow, having lost his breath stopping a fizzing breakback from Johnny, could not (as he could when he was playing other bowlers) take a little walk round the crease and get his lungs full again. No; Briggs bowled ball after ball quicker than any other bowler that ever made batsman's life intolerable. He had no long trek back to his bowling base: a short stride or two, a bounce, and here he was again. And you couldn't jump out to many of his slows, to get them on the half-volley. He seemed to give the ball no upward curve at all: down to the wicket from his arm it came, for all the distraught batsman knew. His fast ball, too, had to be "looked out for." He could bowl "a yard faster" without the faintest change of action.

Still, you would not call him a bowler crafty in the Rhodes and Trumble sense. These men went about their work plainly using fundamental brainwork. You could see them, while they were fielding at mid-off, thinking over problems, considering technical ways and means for the next over. Briggs never gave a hint that he went into moments of abstraction, of private subterfuge. His was nature's cunning; he did the wily thing as Brer Fox does it. His craft worked by instinct, not by reason, and improvisation was the note of it. So, too, when he was making his runs. A characteristic innings by Briggs raced along like a scherzo. His bat flashed impudently. He looked to be always on his toes, "daring" the bowler. Out of his crease would he skip, suggesting a short run, and back home would he scurry as some frantic fieldsman shook the earth with intimidatory thuds. He was, so to say, always "pulling fat bacon" at the field while he batted. Half of his runs he made by an audacious slash at the off-side ball. It was not a cut or a slice, but a combination of both. As the ball passed the wicket he seemed to hit it with a horizontal bat but with the bat's full face. The stroke made everybody laugh—save the man at point who had to get out of the way of it, and the bowler. Something of a miracle happened when Briggs contrived a long innings—as often enough he did. He "played with fire" all the time, and, as it is with the child who plays with fire, Providence usually watched over him. His batsmanship was the triumph of a keen eye and quickly responding muscles. And so was it his sharp sight and agility of body that made him Vernon Royle's successor in the offside field—not in Royle's classical manner, but in a spring-heeled way of his own.

The crowd loved him because he was a comedian. But was he at bottom *always* the laughing cricketer? Look at the photographs of the man. About the mouth there is a droop which does not obviously suggest unwearying high spirits. There is in the eyes the look of a man not born to be funny from morning till night, day in and day out. The old tragedy of the comedian, indeed, was in Briggs, the tragedy of the merry Andrews the world insists must live through their saddest days to the sound of men laughing at them. That droop of Briggs's lips which would come in moments which took him " off his guard " was the grimace of Grimaldi himself. We all of us know now that Briggs must have found, many a day, that it was hard to be funny. He was really a man of uncommon sensibility. His nerves were easily jarred. When he tossed his audacious ball to George Ulyett in the famous Lancashire and Yorkshire match at Old Trafford, and when Ulyett hit it deep to the long field where Albert Ward waited and caught it, the crowd mingled with its tumult of acclamation some rich chuckles at yet another " little dodge of Johnny." But in the pavilion, after the match, poor Briggs sat with a white face. Bowling his " little dodge " had well-nigh burst his heart with apprehension. And the end of his life was as sad as **Jack Point's**. We will perhaps do proper homage to Briggs's memory if, after we have thought of him with a smile—and he would surely like us to smile,—we also think for a moment sadly of him.

CHAPTER XIV

LESSONS FROM LORD'S: THE TWO-EYED STANCE

(*July* 1920)

THE annual engagement between the Great Unpaid and the Workmen always invites a rather more closely technical scrutiny than the county match that gives one an axe of partisanship to grind. The solitary run which won Lancashire the other day a great victory against Hampshire at Liverpool might have been from a woeful mishit. Nobody knows and nobody cares. But this is not the way we look at cricket in a Gentlemen v. Players match. A man is hardly going to get himself hoarse shouting either side home. Perhaps in these days the spread of democratic ideas has tended to make the Players favourites with everybody at Lord's excepting the Dedlocks in the pavilion, but really the backing which either side gets from the crowd is of the faintest. The interest in the Gentlemen and Players match is definitely a technical or a spectacular interest. And it does our great summer pastime vast credit that it attracts crowds so exquisitely aware of the fine shades as the crowd at Lord's last week. Surely no game, unless it be tennis, can boast supporters as intelligent as those which watch cricket.

LESSONS FROM LORD'S

The frenzy of combat not present, then, we are in a position during a Gentlemen v. Players match to witness the play with the detachment of Olympians. And how hypercritical one can become! The men on view at Lord's last week certainly passed through that hell of criticism feared by John Keats. And, truth to tell, they got their deserts, speaking of the mass of them. Only four players escaped hard words —Hobbs, Chapman, Wood and Russell. The others no doubt were beneath themselves. Possibly the occasion rather put a fellow off his game. You see, there were exceptional circumstances attending the match. It was not only the usual ordeal of a representative fixture at Lord's. A player knew he was in the scales, being " weighed in," so to speak, for the Australian journey. Then the Gentlemen had to try and wipe out the discredit of that defeat at the Oval a week or two ago, and the Players could not bear to think of the blot on their reputation which would come if they went down before an amateur side of to-day. These facts we must therefore bring forward in extenuation of much of the bad cricket.

But it is still hard to account for it all. Let us throw in another possible explanation. Every player, even in a successful season, has an " off " day now and again, when he can do nothing right. The greatest of modern batsmen—Hobbs, I mean— explained to me the other day that success " on the middle " often is a mere matter of mood. Some days, as Hobbs said, " a chap doesn't feel like it." Everybody knows that feeling, be he a Prime

Minister or a bricklayer. There are signs of the poet's " off days " even in " Paradise Lost." Well, it is possible that eighteen fine cricketers may let upon their bad moments all in the same match. That conceivably happened at Lord's.

And by now the writer hopes he has given ample evidence of approaching a summing up of the game in a spirit of mercy and charity. He is the freer, therefore, to write down what he considers were the unmistakable blemishes in the play. A cricketer may be out of mood; he may also have dropped on his bad patch for the moment; he may make a " duck " in consequence—but he need not display a faulty technique. A batsman " out of form " is one that scores a few runs, not one that shows us a cross bat, a wrong stance, a misguided method. Shrewsbury frequently got out for next to nothing, but only through some dilatoriness of eye and muscle; rarely if ever because of a hopelessly incorrect technique. And that is just what one cannot say of many cricketers at Lord's in this Gentlemen v. Players match. Too many of them made the schoolboy's mistake of hitting against the break. And despite the fast wicket and the fact that the bowling was usually straight length stuff, they allowed the left shoulder to swing round towards mid-on and the right leg to move over to the off stump *before* the stroke was in swing. It was that curse of modern cricket, the two-eyed stance, working its evil again.

The writer is not one of those who are against this stance at all times and seasons. It did not come

LESSONS FROM LORD'S

into fashion out of the sheer "cussedness" of batsmen. True, the batsmen of the classical epoch rarely used it—William Gunn, Daft, Grace, Palairet, Ford, and the rest. But that was because the bowling of their period did not demand it. The two-eyed stance—hideous name!—means that instead of keeping your left shoulder fairly forward in playing in front of the wicket, you come round or only half round, by a move of the right foot over the wicket, thus enabling the bowler to see your chest but not the stumps, since your pads are in front. This stance helps you to back up with the pads to the breaking ball. Now, in the days of "classical" forward play there were, of course, plenty of breaking balls, but no "googlies." It was the advent of the "googly" which saw the wholesale adoption of the two-eyed stance. Batsmen, not knowing which way the ball was going to turn, could not play forward with the old-time confident lunge of the left leg. That beautiful stroke asked for a ball that gave up its secret in mid-air, for, of course, "classical" forward play had a moment when the batsman lost sight of the ball—just, in fact, as the forward stroke was made. You played "at the pitch" knowing exactly what the ball was going to do. It is no accident that immaculate batting was to be seen on county grounds at the same time as the immaculate length bowling of Alfred Shaw, Attewell, J. T. Hearne, George Lohmann, Peel, Briggs, Trumble, and Howell—to name just a few. The modern craze for finger spin made it pretty necessary for batsmen to get as far back on the wicket as possible, so that the length might be shortened and the ball work off its spin before the stroke was attempted. And as back play behind the right leg is suicidal to a turning ball, the batsman simply had to come round almost square to the bowler. And not only did the " googly " force batsmen into the two-eyed stance; there was also a rage for leg-breaks. Again, the off theory bowled by the Attewell school, with all the field round about point and cover, knocked off-side play on the head. To make runs a man had to pull—and that encouraged the two-eyed stance still further.

Granted certain conditions, then, the two-eyed stance was a legitimate resort. On sticky wickets it is quite necessary. Against bowlers like Vogler, Schwarz, Faulkner, Hordern, and Bettington it goes a long way as a defensive measure. But against straight bowling on a fast wicket, the two-eyed stance cannot be justified. And at Lord's last week we had a fairly fast ground, and, as I have said, straightish bowling. Yet, player after player managed a ball to the off in this way: a move of the right leg to the line of flight and a push at the ball, the right wrist providing the leverage. The off ball treated in this fashion was made into a straight one, and this position taken up by the batsman allowed no more than a defensive stroke. A few years ago a fast off ball would have been dealt with by a fling of the left leg across the wicket, a free swing of the bat, a boundary past cover, the left shoulder pointing in direction of the hit just before the moment of

LESSONS FROM LORD'S

impact and following through after. Why did Hendren try to hook the off ball bowled to him by Jupp on Wednesday? It was simply asking to be hit past cover. Why did the Players score less runs on the off side than on the on side, from the fast medium bowling pitched mainly off the wicket? And how can we call cricketers masters of the hook stroke and the on drive while all the time they are convincing us that they are the slaves of these strokes? How can a man possibly cut or drive past cover if his left shoulder points towards mid-on? And what good is a man against fast bowling of length on a hard ground if he cannot cut or off-drive safely? The two-eyed stance means a cross bat to every forcing hit against balls off the wicket and even against balls on the middle and off stumps. It is safe, probably, on slow turf where the ball hangs after pitching. But on fast wickets from which the ball " fizzes " in like lightning the bat must be straight. In Australia even Jessop could not " hook " on those fast wickets. There you must cut and off-drive, and Foster, Tyldesley, Macartney, Hill, and Hardstaff were masters of these prolific strokes on hard grounds.

It is urgent that we ponder this defect in modern batsmanship just now. The best judges of the game are agreed that it is doing English cricket no good. Yet it is difficult to say what can be done—the fashion must run its course. Cricketers, like Hans Sach's Nuremburgers, will have their midsummer whims. But let us hope that those who have in their trust the coaching of young players to-day will insist on a return to first principles. There are signs that bowlers are going back to good length and accuracy on the off side; a few more Lohmanns and Shaws will settle the two-eyed stance. And if the Australians possess a Trumble to-day he, too, will assist in the good work. An old cricketer at Lord's the other day told me he would not take a batsman to Australia if he were a " two-eyed 'un "—no, not if his average were a hundred an innings over here.

CHAPTER XV

EVOLUTIONS

THE man who would fix the beginning of modern cricket is likely to make the mistake of J. R. Green, who looked for the beginning of modern English history and found it three times. Did the modern game set in with the first ball sent down overhand? A case (for the purposes of an armchair argument) might be made for the notion. The advent of bowling delivered with the arm above the shoulder must, to say the least, have caused a revolution in the game the like of which can rarely have been known to cricketers before or after Willsher, of Kent, the most notable pioneer of overarm bowling. It was June, 1864, before the M.C.C. legalised overhead bowling—" cartwheel " stuff as the purists of the day called it. In the Hambledon era lobs were the fashion—though not the twisting things we of to-day call lobs, with Jephson, Simpson-Hayward, and Walter Humphreys in mind. John Nyren, the high poet of Hambledon, said of a bowler that he must cultivate " a proper length," but advised young cricketers not to attempt " twist." Underarm bowling in those days was often fast. How did the Hambledon men achieve their pace with an action which modern bowlers would find inadequate in swing and body energy? Would the Hambledon fast bowling seem fast to us, who have watched Richardson, Brearley, Kortright, and Ernest Jones ? There is positive evidence that the old lob bowlers were fast. Osbaldeston was the terror not only of batsmen but of longstops, and Brown, of Brighton, needed three longstops, and once he beat the lot of them with a ball that killed a dog on the boundary. The famous lob bowlers of that age (we see it through the enchanting mists of distance!) were Lumpy, Frame, David Harris, " tall and upright as a Grenadier," and (one must not forget this one) Mr Luffey, who bowled in the match which Mr Pickwick witnessed. Mr Luffey, we are informed by Dickens, retired a few paces behind the wicket and applied the ball to his right eye for several minutes, and then cried " Play " in a fierce voice. But one must hasten to add that Dickens's impression of a cricket match of the 'thirties must not be taken as quite authentic. For Dickens the glory of life was energy, and where he could not find it in fact his imagination provided it. Thus even a tranquil game in an old England meadow he must transform into a whirling, agitated mob—batsmen stunning themselves in collision, bowlers beside themselves with excitement, and the fieldsmen bruised and bleeding through catching the ball on their skulls. Cricket in the 'thirties was an elegant game; does not Nyren himself call it the " manly and elegant game of cricket " ? That men could play it and wear tophats at the same time speaks eloquently enough of the poise and dignity of the old cricketers.

The " bridge " between the Hambledon and

EVOLUTIONS

modern bowling was the " round arm " manner, invented in 1787 by Tom Walker, but not sanctioned by law till some forty years afterwards. We must give Walker his due, even at the expense of the pretty tale which would have us believe a certain Mr Willes hit upon the " round arm " way through watching his sister bowl. The " new bowling " became the rage in 1827, when a Sussex team, with Lillywhite in it, made use of " round arms " and thrashed England twice out of three matches. And for thirty years round-arm bowling was the recognised technique in first-class company. The rough wickets no doubt gave it a sting it would not have on modern grounds; still, Wootton, Tarrant, Wisden, Caffyn, and Alfred Mynn brought to the style genius of their own. There was little or no slow round-arm bowling; it was fast or fast medium. Not to be too sentimental about old-time cricket, let one say there is reason to believe bowling in the round-arm period often fell far below an artistic level. Even Frederick Gale had to admit that much of the round-arm bowling was " rubbish." The very action of the round arm is against a varied attack, and so long as it was the fashion there could be no great chance of spin or flight variation. The off-break, for instance, cannot be easily bowled with the arm no higher than the shoulder.

The game turned top over heels, so to say, with the coming of overarms. The ball now went to the batsman from a height that permitted subtler flight variations than the round-arm men could even attempt;

also, the overarm action had its natural spin and pace from the pitch to set the batsmen a-dancing. Batsmanship, indeed, had to begin all over again, footwork elaborated, and new defensive as well as offensive strokes invented. And as batsmen worked out a new technique, the field had to be set in a new way. Not all at once, of course, did overarm bowling ring the changes: for a while it was not much more subtle than the round-arm stuff itself. Wickets still were dangerous, and a bowler could get his victims without the wear and tear of grey matter. Then the arts of the groundsmen came more and more to perfection. After all, maybe the most violent revolution in cricket history was caused by the application of heavy roller and mowing machine to wickets—as Mr Lyttelton has suggested. As more and more level grounds were made, batsmen began to gain mastery even over the formidable over-arms. Then the bowlers *had* to think. Moreover the greatest of all cricketers was beginning to fix the mark of his genius on the technique of batsmanship. W. G. Grace invented modern batting and, as much as the safer grounds, killed or half-killed the " brute force " bowlers. On the improved wickets he flogged fast bowling to his heart's content. Moreover, there were keen disciples of the master's methods up and down the land. The battle of wits between batsman and bowler—and the history of cricket is one long battle of wits between them—went on, and by 1877 scores of bowlers had gone to the opposite extreme of the Jackson and Willsher school, and were bowling slows.

EVOLUTIONS

Was not the time now ripe for the really great modern bowler? The problem was there for him to solve—Grace on a tolerably good pitch. And the materials of the modern bowler were there (save the googly!), though they were distributed amongst many men, none of them quite master of *all* the tricks. Whoever should come at this "psychological" moment and sum up in his own art all the scattered elements, he would surely be hailed the first of the great bowlers of modern cricket history.

He did come—most promptly to his cue, his name Spofforth. Before his heyday there were fast bowlers, slow bowlers, and medium-paced bowlers, but hardly a solitary cricketer who combined in his own bowling all the paces and all the breaks. Spofforth's fame is abused if we think of him merely as a fast bowler. At his greatest he was a master af variations, with a slow ball as deadly as his fastest. If one believes only half the tales that are told by the old men of Spofforth's prowess, one is forced to think that no bowler since Spofforth has had quite his genius. None of the resources of the bowler of to-day were unknown to Spofforth—save the googly, whose contribution to the art hardly looks permanent just now. It would seem he exhausted the potentialities of overarm bowling which are really worth while, and the problem of bowlers of to-day is to improve on his craft.

It cannot be said that Grace so completely as this touched in batsmanship the perfection that gives the sense of finality. It is true he invented modern batting; true, too, that, as Ranjitsinhji said, he changed batting from an accomplishment into a science. But did he quite make it the fine art that it was in Trumper's hands, in Ranji's hands? He was the greatest run-making machine ever known, but did he, through batsmanship, convey so much of beauty as Spooner? One reads that Grace, almost to the end, obeyed the old law which discountenanced the mobile right foot. Well, think of the thrilling agility of Trumper, and ask how could Grace have so stirred the imagination, the æsthetic sense, as Trumper did? And poor indeed would have been the service done to the Great Old Man's genius had not the batsmen who followed him seen that the lessons taught by him were not barren, but fruitful. " He turned the old one-stringed instrument into a many-chorded lyre," wrote Ranjitsinhji of Grace. And Ranji, Trumper, and Spooner made music out of it surely more beautiful than ever the old cricketers knew. Is it blasphemous to say so much? Tales of Silver Billy Beldham, of Pilch, of Carpenter, of Daft, of Shrewsbury and Gunn, of Lucas—down the ages come tales of how much of beauty these artists put into cricket. Well, the poor modern cricketer must say something in defence against the cry " The game is not what it used to be ! " He will admit that, as a contest, cricket to-day probably cannot compare with the game as it was when a great batsman had to face a great bowler. He will admit that bowling has not advanced in lasting points since Spofforth. He will even admit that since the war cricket in the lump has fallen away

EVOLUTIONS

abominably. But he cannot (at least the writer cannot) believe that batsmanship ever had style more varied than in the 1902-12 period, or beauty with so much temperament in it. It may even be said that the great batsmen of the 1902-12 period fell so completely in love with the notion of batsmanship as an art through which personality might be expressed that they forgot cricket was a game. It may even be said these modern masters were selfish, but, if so, their selfishness was just the defect of the artistic temperament. Give modern batsmanship its due. The art of Hayward was not less immaculate, not less classic in its calm poise, than Daft's; yet he might have been seen and admired on the same day that saw Jessop riding the whirlwind. Spooner gave us glimpses into loveliness too frail to last—he was the Herrick of batsmen. And yet he expressed himself through the same means that served MacLaren, whose batsmanship might well have been that of a Roman Emperor of the decadence. And Ranji there was letting in on our English game a light from the East, yet Hirst, too, using the same game to express his comfortable rusticity—a Hambledonian, here, if ever there lived one. Give modern cricket its due indeed. The old men who speak eternally of its deterioration do scant homage to the cricketers of the past. Theirs was the sowing—and no modern cricketer at least (if he will only forget the present temporary blight cast by the war) is going to say the harvest has been inglorious.

CHAPTER XVI

COOK OF LANCASHIRE

(*August* 1921)

THE ways of Selection Committees in English cricket possess a most notable habit of procrastination. Even the making of a Test match eleven is dawdled over till the last minute. The merit of a cricketer, seemingly, needs to be a very Bardolph's nose of obviousness before it lights the ways that Selection Committees move along. Let us count it a blessing, though, that in the judgment seats at Lord's they at least can be " wise in time." They even in time discovered the merit of Cook and invited him definitely to bowl for the Players. As long ago as last summer any amount of good critics of the game agreed that Cook was our very best right-arm medium-paced length bowler. Still, though Cook's bowling overthrew some 150 batsmen in 1920 you rarely found his name spoken in the South of England on those occasions when the picking of representative cricket teams was the pastime. No—you would hear the London folk playing, as usual, the parrot with " Hobbs, Hearne, Hendren, Woolley," and the rest, and how pained would they look at an interruption " How about Cook ? " Cook, though he was in the very first flight of our bowlers in 1920 even at

COOK OF LANCASHIRE

the time the Players' eleven at Lord's was chosen, did not play in the match. But he was "twelfth man" and so, like the poet who got sick of eternal comparison with Victor Hugo, he had the privilege of saying, "Thank God, I'm at least a contemporary." Cook, despite that the game's richest laurels did not come his direction, went his honourable way for Lancashire. This summer, on hard grounds that have been all against his art, he has taken 91 wickets up to the moment of writing, and now, at long last, as we have seen, the powers at Lord's have thoroughly grasped the fact of his continued existence and ability.

A cynic might observe of Cook that he works too hard to be a man with anything of genius in him. The modern notion of genius has little reverence for Carlyle's "infinite capacity for taking pains." "Inspiration," whatever that may mean in the popular sense, is nowadays the fashionable attribute of genius. Well, Cook himself would not claim that he has genius, nor would even his best critics, but if ever a man possessed an infinite capacity for taking pains, it is Cook. Cook, indeed perhaps more than any other cricketer in the game to-day, would move a Carlyle to admiration—supposing, in a moment of fancy, Carlyle interested in modern cricket at all. "Thou honest man," we can imagine him saying, as he witnessed Cook toiling under the melting sun, "Thou art too honest in toil for the fashionable places and their titles of honour. Yet toil on; *thou art in thy duty, be out of it who may!*" Cook is,

A CRICKETER'S BOOK

in fact, a great toiler before he is anything else: the man in the crowd, with his customary fine instinct after a sound classification of players of games, will describe Cook to you as first of all " a worker." The writer occasionally has a notion that Cook is of the progeny of Tim Linkinwater, the industrious and loyal servant of the Cheerybles, and that a full-toss on the leg side is for Cook just as terrible a crime as a blot in his ledger was for Tim Linkinwater. In a world where everybody lived in his proper dramatic setting Cook most certainly would serve, and serve faithfully, the Cheerybles, who, of course, would have been lovers of cricket had they lived to-day—and in daily attendance on the pavilion at Old Trafford. And cannot you imagine these Cheerybles coming upon Cook some scorching afternoon and growling at him: " Where's that scoundrel Cook? Why, brother, here he's been bowling for two hours at a stretch, and had the impudence to get six wickets for 52 runs. Cook, you villain, take a month's holiday at once ! "

But it is not hard labour alone that has got Cook on in the world; he is not of those undistinguished toilers needing the doubtful solace of Kingsley's " let who will be clever." Cook *is* clever—he is one of the cleverest cricketers in the country. With him cleverness and industry go, for once in a way, together. We have seen that Cook can point to notable bowling figures. But, of course, averages do not tell everything—though they are often mistakenly undervalued as means of assessing a cricketer's quality. At

COOK OF LANCASHIRE

any rate the best bowlers invariably have good averages! Of Cook, though, figures cannot tell you that he is at least two bowlers rolled into one—a man for sticky wickets and a man for hard wickets. With rain about, he is not unlike Schofield Haigh; he bowls a slowish off-break from round the wicket. On a fast ground he can work up a capital pace, but his fastest ball is never over-done. He can whip it down without an obvious change from the action that controls his medium ball. With the ground hard Cook usually begins with a few fashionable swingers. Even this vastly overrated ball he manages in his own way. It is not flighted quite as much as the average swinger—say, that of Robinson of Yorkshire; it is not, in fact, so much a swinger as a ball that goes "with a bowler's arm" from the leg and middle stump to the off. Cook's arm drops ever so slightly when he bowls this ball, and the line of flight is altered from above and straight down the wicket to a point from a little to the right of the bowler's wicket, thence obliquely to the off stump. The ball is likely to hit the off stump or to land in the hands of fine slip, and it may have all the terrors of the swerve to a batsman weak on the off side without taking on the authentic swerve's risk of coming along over-pitched. Cook sends down fewer over-tossed ones than any bowler I have seen this summer. One danger of this swinging ball of Cook's is that, since it can be bowled at a good pace with a low flight, it is not to be easily picked out from a straight ball or a break-back.

A CRICKETER'S BOOK

There is another curious point about Cook's bowling which must worry all but the quickest-eyed batsmen. The swing-over of his arm is likely to suggest a length rather on the short side, when as a fact it happens to be not short at all. Arnold, of Worcestershire, had this characteristic in his bowling, and Cook has it most when, like Arnold, his arm is high and straight over and the ball takes a steep downward course to the pitch. The ball actually drops a good length, but because of the higher elevation at the beginning of the flight the incautious batsman sniffs a short one and does not get far enough forward with his stroke.

It is possible that Cook is little aware of the fine shades in his work—he is one of those that build wiser than they know. The lack of niggling artifice in his work "dates" Cook definitely with the old school of bowlers. And one article of faith in the old school was that there were wickets somewhere behind the batsman's defence—wickets to be hit, for all the width of bat in the world. Nowadays there is a sort of Machiavellian philosophy which insists that a batsman will get himself out if left long enough to himself. Not for Cook—or the old bowlers —this plausible stuff. He is for ever attacking the wicket, worrying the defence, seeking the holes in it. He hits the stumps as frequently as any other bowler in first-class cricket. It is because Cook is invariably "on the wicket" that you may hear so many times in an afternoon that high-pitched and excited appeal of his for "l.b.w." Accuracy in length and direction are the main attributes of Cook's bowling, and they are rare enough in these times.

He is, as the man in the crowd says, " a character." There is a likeable humanity in him. He has the amount of flesh that makes for fellow-feeling. For many years to come Old Trafford will recollect his aspect during this season of heat—the mind's eye will keep the image of him walking back time after time to the place he bowls from, his flannels loose, his fingers screwing the ball round and round, his head slightly on one side,—expressing immense patience in hard toil.

CHAPTER XVII

THE FASHIONABLE BOWLING

(*June* 1920)

CRICKET goes along by fashion hardly less than the ladies' wardrobe. One day we have the leg break on the brain, and the " cow " shot; the next day it is " googlies " or the " off theory." Just now you can hardly walk on to a county ground without finding a bowler who is " swinging " the ball. I do not mean simply the ball that goes with the arm, but the authentic " curler " in the air. Robinson, Calthorpe, Kennedy, Howell, Waddington, Gunasekara —here are just a few who are experts at curling in the air. In a Lancashire match the other day I noticed Makepeace wheeling up a few overs to James Tyldesley during the intervals between the fall of wickets, and even he was swinging a foot. In fact, everybody's doing it. They also swerve who only stand and wait.

But cricketers are such canny empiricists. They will not tell you in abstract terms how a thing is done, only how they individually do it. A classic definition of the swerve or swinger runs in some such way as this. A ball which has check spin on it loses it through friction against the air during flight. At

THE FASHIONABLE BOWLING

this moment the ball slips the air cushion it has made. The check spin keeps the ball with the seam vertical, until the air resistance causes the spin to cease altogether. The wind then " taps " the seam to a slant, and at this point, especially if the ball has an upward tendency and the earth's power of attraction is asserting itself, the swerve begins. Even this highly technical jargon hardly carries us a long way; one thinks of the gentleman in Molière who, asked to explain transparency, said it was something so constituted that you could see through it. The perplexing thing about the swerve is that with some bowlers it will operate even when there is no cross wind to " tap " against the seam. George Hirst, the greatest swerver of all, knew little enough of the way it was done, except that it happened when he held the seam vertically between the first and second fingers, with the side of the thumb underneath the ball. And, to confuse matters, he could not swerve at all in Australia, though he altered his grip and swing not a jot. Of one fact about the swinger, though, we can be tolerably sure. It will operate only on a ball which has a " lot of air "; in other words, which takes a wide flight. Even here one hesitates to dogmatise, for Gunasekara swings with quite a low trajectory. But the axiom will hold good, speaking generally; we must not allow one solitary fact to upset a beautiful generalisation! And this demand of the swerve for a spacious flight in the air is the cause of a vast deal of over-tossing from bowlers nowadays. Never was there such a constant supply of half-volleys sent down in first-class cricket as you can find to-day. Sir Timothy O'Brien, a cricketer of the age of immaculate length bowling, expressed his opinion a few years ago that the craze for swerving, with its resultant overpitching, made bowling a sport for children. He did something to justify this violent notion by coming out of retirement and smiting an innings of ninety or so, after which he went back into his shell, no doubt highly satisfied. Of course his charge against " swervers " in the lump was true; they must needs send full-tosses along in plenty, in order to keep the ball in the air long enough for it to lose its spin, which, as we have seen, has to happen before the ball can slip the air cushion. But Sir Timothy O'Brien did not meet the " crack " swervers, who have solved this problem of the spacious curve very ingeniously. Take M. A. Noble, for instance. Realising that a ball will curl only after it has been in the air a longish time, and that the great thing is to be able to swerve without presenting your batsman a gift of a nice half-volley, Noble got the necessary addition to his curve in the air at *his* end of the wicket—not at the batsman's. He went down slightly by bending the right knee as the arm came over, and at the same time released the ball from the hand farther back than usual in the swing. The ball was thus impelled from a conveniently low altitude; the upward trajectory was consequently a little higher than the average. And so the ball gained that " extra air " in which to lose check spin well away from the batsman's reach; Noble's swerve, indeed, pitched an astonishingly good

THE FASHIONABLE BOWLING

length. It may be true that Noble himself did not consciously manage all these subtleties, no more than Leonardo consciously put into the " Mona Lisa " all those fine shades discovered by Walter Pater. Yet there they were for cricketers to see.

Unfortunately few of our " swingers " to-day are Nobles. The amount of half-volleys they wheel up is so appalling that no more scathing commentary upon the decline of off play in modern cricket could be instanced than that the bulk of these swinging bowlers have quite pleasant analyses just now. The swerve of a right-hander like Robinson goes away towards slip; the co-operation of a batsman who is weak on the cut and cover drive is needed if such a bowler is to be successful. Few right-handers have bowled the really deadly swerve—that which swings in from the off on to the leg stump. J. B. King, the Philadelphian master, could do so. A great cricketer this, whose record in Test Matches, had he been an Englishman or an Australian, would have assured him a sturdy immortality. So, too, can Kennedy, of Hampshire, swing in to the batsman. But this dangerous swerve comes easiest to a left-hander, and, as everybody knows, Hirst was a master with it. The " in " swinger cannot be left alone; it makes for the leg stump. Yet if you play it, what about those three short legs, set like slips? Dean's swinger, in his Test Match period, was of the Hirst type. It is the only swerve really worth cultivating —unless one can get an assurance from somewhere that batting is never again to show mastery over off-driving and cutting. And for those who like to worry out problems of cause and effect I would put forward this teaser: Which came first, the decline in off-side play or the swerve? This is quite as good a breakfast table problem as that old one about the hen and the egg.

CHAPTER XVIII

TOM HAYWARD (1919)

DURING the confusions of war (and of reconstruction) a great cricketer passed out of the game with hardly a voice raised in the land to bid him farewell. Only a few of the zealots, those who keep an affectionate eye on cricket in season and out, paid him due homage. Yet Thomas Hayward was indubitably one of the greatest batsmen of all time. The statisticians, indeed, could place him second to " W. G." himself. For Hayward comes next to the Grand Old Man in the list of the most prolific scorers; his aggregate in all first-class matches was 43,509, as against Grace's 54,896. The " champion " hit 120 centuries, Hayward 104. No other cricketer has gone the full circle of the hundred hundreds. Hayward's batting average for his career is 41.70, which is even higher than " W. G.'s," though we must bear in mind that Hayward was a product of the modern wicket, and probably did not have to withstand in the whole of his cricketing experience as many " shooters " as Grace mastered in that single afternoon at Lord's during the 'seventies, when Morley sent down an over full of them, after which the crowd rose as a man and cheered the great batsman. Hayward is now coach at Oxford University, and as he is in his forty-eighth year it may be taken for granted that the curtain has descended finally on his first-class career.

Hayward was in the direct line of descent from the classical period. He reminded one of Fuller Pilch, and of the age in which man insisted that cricket should be a beautiful as well as a skilful and combative game. It was the period we can visualise nowadays only by the aid of the old prints that depict a gentleman with curly moustaches and sidewhiskers making elaborate movements with a gracefully curved bat, to the admiration of a fashionable company of ladies and gentlemen, all of them congregated in the region of the field occupied nowadays by second slip. Those were the times when cricketers spoke not only of the big hit, but of the sweet, the exquisite hit. So elegant was the motion of cricketers then that they could sustain throughout the heat and burden of the longest day the tall hat with perfect deportment. And the nicest compliment to be offered to Hayward's batting is that in any one of his innings, no matter how tense the struggle under the highly combative modern conditions, he, too, could have worn a tall hat becomingly, had fashion demanded, so effortless was his action, so balanced his poise. The fastest bowling, on the bumpiest pitches, left Hayward unruffled. Only MacLaren had a tithe of his imperial manner. There was, indeed, in MacLaren's cricket an abandon that suggested decadence. Hayward was eminently classic. The modern cry is " 'It 'em 'ard, 'it 'em 'igh, and 'it 'em often." Hayward hit them often enough; he hit them hard. Never did he hit them high. No batsman gave less encouragement to the fielders. The mechanism of his strokes was so precise that his strongest drive sent the ball along the grass. There was no suspicion of the " pull " in his hitting to the on-side. His drive was made well forward on the toes, as may be seen in Mr Beldam's action photographs, with even an off-side lean of the upper part of the body. But one thinks of no particular stroke in Hayward's repertoire. He knew them all, even to the late cut, which has almost disappeared in recent years. His command over forward and back play was so masterful that he was, at his best, the most difficult man in the country to bowl out. It is the sheerest myth to suggest, as some of Hayward's critics did suggest, that he was a " fair weather " batsman, the spoiled child of Apted, who made lovely wickets at the Oval. In 1903, which was the wettest summer since 1879, Hayward scored over 2,000 runs, with an average of 37. Lancashire cricketers will recollect his innings at Old Trafford in 1914, when he scored 76 after A. H. Hornby sent Surrey in first.

Of course, his best work was done on good fast wickets—he was only like other great batsmen in this respect. His most wonderful season was 1906. He then amassed the record individual aggregate for a single summer:—3,518; average 66.37. He also scored thirteen centuries, a feat equalled in first-class cricket by C. B. Fry and nobody else. In Whit week 1906 Hayward scored 144 not out and 100 at Nottingham, and 148 and 125 at Leicester, bringing off the batsman's "double" in two successive matches. This remarkable cricket took us back to those majestic days of May, 1895, when "W. G." scored 1,000 runs in the month, completing only nine innings and averaging 112. It is good to think that Hayward is spending the closing days of his career instructing the young idea in the principles of the game. The heartiest wishes of all cricketers go with him in his new work, which, we may be sure, will bear good fruit in time.

CHAPTER XIX

SPOONER AT OLD TRAFFORD

(*August* 1920)

THE innings of Spooner in the Lancashire and Yorkshire match on August Bank Holiday will not quickly be forgotten. It was his return to the crowd that loves him after a long absence, and the magic of his art made everybody on the packed ground that day into a jubilant, shouting schoolboy. Such batsmanship had not been seen at Old Trafford since the Augustan days before the war. He went in first with Heap. Waddington gave him some trouble before he found the pace of the drying turf. We hung on to his every movement. If he should fail! Ah, be careful Reggie with that swinging off-ball! For a while we sit in purgatory. And then the master drives Waddington gloriously to the on-boundary, and we are in paradise. The master is now in tune with himself. Two off drives to the rails from successive balls off Rhodes—and then the sheerest poetry of cricket. " Wrist-work! Wrist-work! " is the usual comment on Spooner's cricket. And it really does seem that he makes his forcing strokes even as an artistic housemaid uses a feather-duster. But no man could urge a ball in front of the wicket, with Spooner's strength, by wrist-work alone. There must be some latent body energy in the hit; the muscular mechanism works so smoothly that it deceives us. A fountain is a thing of fairy spray to the eye, but underground some violent pressure goes on. It may be in such wise with Spooner's batsmanship.

The great man in cricket, as in all other arts, is an individualist, whose game is as much a part of him as his physiognomy (to echo Fenélon), his figure, his throbbing pulse—in short, as any part of his being which is subjected to the action of the will. In and through the art of batsmanship we have come to know Spooner as intimately as if he had written Sonnets to a Dark Lady. Walk at random on a cricket field and see Spooner make his off-drive. You have no need to be informed that Spooner is batting. The stroke can be " attributed " with as much certainty as any canvas by Paul Véronèse. That graceful forward poise, the supple play of the wrists! Ranji himself was not more graceful than Spooner. There was, in fact, a disturbing melodramatic element in Ranji now and then. When he glanced to leg that straight fast ball dead on the middle stump, you gasped amazedly. And emotion is never pricked as sharply as that by sheer grace. In Spooner's batting, at his best, we see the unities observed (as the gentleman in Dickens would say); the harmony, the eternal fitness of the game, suffers no shock. For Spooner just puts a bloom on the orthodox. His cricket has a classical

SPOONER AT OLD TRAFFORD

purity in these days. But if his decorative formality makes him a Pre-Raphaelite, so to say, he is a Pre-Raphaelite of the Millais order,—the Millais who painted "Autumn Leaves." There is warm colour in his play as well as the clear natural outlines.

CHAPTER XX

RHODES—A STUDY

(*August* 1920)

THE Lancashire and Yorkshire match gave us not only the batting of Spooner. On the closing day we had some beautiful bowling by Rhodes. It is possible that the memory will before long find itself unable to hold a lot of the things we talked most about as we watched the cricket last week, but surely the sight of Spooner and Rhodes in conflict—and both at their greatest—made an impression that is not going to be wiped out by a hundred days' common impingement on the mind. Let old cricketers hug recollections of Spofforth tackling the Grand Old Man; of Lockwood and Ranji in antagonism. Here, at Old Trafford, we had a spectacle just as fit for the fighting gods—the most charming of all batsmen pitting his art against the cleverest of modern bowlers. Rhodes won at the finish, but he had to brood on his problem for two hours. Yet how like nectar must have been the taste of his victory in the mouth! Had he not at long last drawn—nay sucked—Spooner out of his crease, as he had plainly said he would do from the moment he first bowled at him? That is the marvellous fact about Rhodes's

RHODES

method; he announces his intentions for the whole field to heed. "That is your favourite stroke is it?" he seems to say to the batsman. "Good! I challenge you on it—I'll make you go to the well once too often!" Skill for skill in the light of open day, his motto may well be. No googlies for Rhodes, no "mystery" bowling. Just the good old-fashioned length, variations, and spin stuff managed by a master.

A matter of immense skill is this slow bowling. Unless it be clever, a schoolboy will play it. The fast bowler can get you out with a long hop; there is the unnerving element of sheer pace to assist him. Even your medium-paced bowler owes a little to what George Lohmann called "brute strength." Slow bowling is "absolute"—as the musicians would say—bowling whose first and last attribute is skill. Watch Rhodes from the ring and you cannot but ask why the man with the bat doesn't jump out and hit the ball before it pitches. It seems so simple. Yet the poor man is standing there for all the world as though the ball were going to explode as soon as it touched the ground. See him lunging forward, extended absurdly, while Dolphin can hardly contain himself, so eager is he to whisk off the bails immediately Rhodes draws his victim over the crease.

What is the secret of this bowling which looks innocence itself? Spin, you say? Well, Rhodes has been able to spin the ball in his time with any man alive. Yet did he not work great destruction in

Australia, with Warner's first XI., on grounds which will not take a slow bowler's spin? There was a Test Match played at Sydney in December, 1903, on a perfect wicket. The turf was as hard as iron; its surface shone like an ironed shirt-front. Impossible to spin a ball here. And the might of Australia in her greatest period passed before Rhodes that broiling day—Trumper, Duff, Hill, Noble, Armstrong, Gregory—all of them amongst the world's greatest batsmen. Australia scored 485, and this was Rhodes' bowling analysis: 48 overs, 94 runs, 5 wickets. Is there anything in the annals of the great bowlers of all time to beat that? Trumper made 185 not out, but Rhodes kept him on the defensive always. And Rhodes could not turn the ball on that wicket: he did it all by slow bowling of good length, and cleverly exploited flight variations. Variations of flight! Here we are at the core of the matter. Many bowlers have there been quite as clever as Rhodes at spinning a ball—W. C. Smith, Wainwright, King (of Leicestershire), Hallam, J. N. Crawford, to name just a few at random. But great batsmen are not likely to be worried by break alone if they are in *no doubt while the ball is in the air*. The great slow bowler gets his men out before the ball pitches; spin with him is simply an accessory after the act.

The problem facing the slow bowler is how to combine with his pace a length which the batsman cannot reach in comfortable time. Usually a slow ball asks for a wide curve in the air, and this the quick-

RHODES

footed batsman can jump to. Try for yourself to bowl a pace under medium without over-tossing. Try to combine, as Rhodes does, a pace which is slow enough to take any amount of spin, with a length short enough to keep you in that terrible mental state known as " between two minds "—try to do this, and you will understand right away what it is that makes Rhodes the greatest of slow bowlers on all wickets. Rhodes bowls a tantalisingly slow pace with the moderately low flight of a J. T. Hearne. And so you get a spinning ball that forbids the quick-footed jump to the pitch—which is the best way of coping with a slow ball. And because his slow ball takes a low flight it is difficult to see his faster ball. The average bowler of Rhodes's pace is compelled to toss his slow ball so high in the air that the lower flight of his fast one—and, of course, all fast bowling must come along with a tolerably low flight—gives ample warning of the change.

A deceptive flight, then, is the secret of Rhodes's art. His spin—the accessory after the act—makes matters worse for the batsman, of course. A left-hander's off-break is a horrid affair at any time. The ball is bowled from outside the line between wicket and wicket and swings into the batsman. Then after pitching it whips away along a transverse diagonal. That is to say, the direction of the ball in the air is in contrast to the direction of the break. Now, supposing with this off-break you get a ball cunningly concealed which does not whip away but goes right through. How can you make up your mind whether to play "inside" or "outside" the line of flight? Rhodes mixes the ball that goes right through with the one that breaks away, and so skilfully does he conceal "t'other from which" that he gets most of his men out by slip catches, l.b.w., and caught at the wicket.

His action is easy and rhythmic. A short run—nay, it is just a walk—and the body goes back over the left leg. The batsman sees the bowler's side just before the arm comes over with a lovely sweep. It is surely the best-known bowling action on the cricket field to-day, now that Hirst has done with his old hop, skip and jump. Rhodes has been bowling since 1898. A few years ago he conceived an ambition to go in first for England as batsman. (He had until then been No. 11 on the order of going in for Test matches). Rhodes applied himself diligently to the business of making runs, and lived not only to go in with Hobbs against Australia but to help Hobbs establish the Test match record of 839 for the first wicket. Meanwhile Rhodes allowed his bowling to rust. On his last visit to Australia (1912) he bowled only 18 overs in Test matches, and took one wicket. During the war, though, Yorkshire lost Booth and Drake, two great bowlers. No youngsters came along to take their places. And Haigh gave up the first-class game. Yorkshire wanted wickets, and that was enough for Rhodes. He returned to the point where he had left his bowling some ten years before, and picked it all up, as though he had never dropped it for a moment. It all reads like a fairy tale. To-day he is again at the top of the bowling averages. Why doesn't somebody call Rhodes the Peter Pan of cricket?

CHAPTER XXI

PARKIN AND HIS BOWLING

(*July* 1920)

A FAMOUS batsman who can speak from first-hand experience of Parkin's bowling told me the other day that he does not bowl you out—" he fools you out ! " This remark gives a deal of force to a comment made on Parkin by a London critic who suggested that if he played first-class cricket day by day batsmen might get to know his tricks and come in time to master him.

There is no doubt that Parkin is essentially a " mystery " bowler, an Artful Dodger, whose success depends very largely on your not knowing exactly what his sleeve conceals. And it is true also that we can hardly say this of most great bowlers. Never was a more frank, a more open attack than Alfred Shaw's. A consistent length, the faintest suggestion of an off-break now and then. " I will not deceive you," we can imagine him as saying, like the old lady in Dickens. Yet he bowled out the best batsmen of his period year after year. It was with him a case of technique challenging technique in the light of open day. And in our time we have seen George Hirst take his 200 wickets by methods as open and as guileless as his own magnificent Yorkshire smile.

PARKIN AND HIS BOWLING

His tactics were announced by that elaborate field on the leg side; had a man with a bell gone round the ground before the match announcing that Hirst was about to bowl his famous in-swinger, the intentions of this great cricketer could not have been made plainer. None the less Hirst on his day was a match for C. B. Fry on his. The ball he bowled had what the metaphysician would call an absolute quality of unplayableness; it did not require that you should be just taken off your guard.

So, too, was it with Richardson's break-back. A batsman knew it was coming as soon as he saw the familiar lithe run to the wicket, that bend to the off-side of the upper body over the left leg, that thrilling sweep of the right arm across the line of flight. None the less, the batsman's " preparedness " was of no avail. The ball came along like a shot from a gun, and lucky man you if there was not the old sickening rattle behind you, followed by a vision of the wicket-keeper swinging his gloves rhythmically across the chest the while he gazed contemplatively at the shattered stumps.

Parkin's bowling certainly has not this technical self-sufficiency. Take an over from him and examine it ball by ball and you will find very few out-of-the-way qualities about them. His fast one is good, and so is his break-back, but *qua* fast ball and *qua* break-back there is nothing unique in either. Parkin, in fact, gets plenty of men out by bad balls—half-volleys and long hops. You must look at his bowling in sequence to understand how he does it all. In the right context, so to speak, even a full toss is difficult to play.

At the Oval the other week Parkin sent up a well-pitched one to Fender, who hit it for six. He promptly gave Fender another, which was almost a full toss. But it was faster and it wrecked the wicket. Parkin mixes them so promiscuously that to a batsman just a little overtsrung by the occasion the effect is thoroughly unsettling. Imagine yourself in a big match, not quite hardened to an " occasion." You arrive at the wicket conscious of that feeling of slight weakness at the knees. Everything around you looks frightfully big, the wickets, the stumper and his pads. The bowler is a giant, and you notice as you pass him on the way to the crease that there are hairs on his arms. Better by far, at such a time of ordeal, one of those steady length bowlers ! How can you trust this Parkin and his full tosses that positively sing with finger spin, and his apparent half-volleys that drop a foot shorter than any decent half-volley ought to do ! Then Parkin is so tenacious; surely some psychological factor enters into his work. He is convinced he can get you out; and there are ten men all around with large hands eager to help him.

But though a bowler can fool some batsmen all the time, can he fool every batsman all the time—especially a case-hardened Test match cricketer who has no nerves ? That is the bone of contention in every discussion to-day * about Parkin. Is it not conceiv-

* This, remember, was written in 1920 before Parkin had been " exposed " by Macartney & Co.

PARKIN AND HIS BOWLING

able that batsmen might find some of his tricks a little commonplace, granted a peep into his bag every day? A good many cricketers at the present time declare that if one could just get " used " to his changefulness, there is nothing essential about his bowling to worry over. As we have seen, a great bowler trusts to sheer technical mastery; could Parkin continue to defeat resourceful batsmen once they had made themselves familiar with his " mixtures? " Time alone can settle this issue. My own view is that one could write more confidently of Parkin's future in big cricket if he had given a stronger impression than he has done so far that he manages his variations with a proper understanding of a batsman's weak points, and according to a logical and purposeful plan. Every time I have seen Parkin bowl I have felt his variations were piecemeal, just opportunist—a fast ball now, a slow ball now, now a leg-break, now an off-break, all on the spur of the moment. That is not quite the way of the subtle bowler, and a wise batsman would not be long, once the novelty of it all was over, in finding out its weakness. He would then treat each ball strictly on its merits, knowing well that there was really no deep-laid plot behind that over-tossed off-ball. Variations handled by a master are mere camouflage to the ball which the bowler has decided, after a good deal of fundamental brainwork, will break through the batsman's weak spot. George Lohmann did not conduct his variations in any haphazard fashion from ball to ball, but over a long spell of work. Johnny Briggs might

A CRICKETER'S BOOK

come in, eager to exploit his curious slash stroke past mid-off, made with a horizontal bat. Lohmann would give him a half-volley, and even another. That was the bait. Then, slowly and imperceptibly, the length was shortened on the off-side; one or two diversions in the form of leg-breaks, fast straight ones, and so on, were sandwiched into the overs just to take the batsman's attention away from the main purpose. But all the time the off-ball was going up, apparently feeding Briggs's risky cover drive, and in good time Lohmann played his trump—a ball very like that which Briggs so loved to hit, but in reality a lot shorter and whipping away as the bat came down. And so the batsman had to go from a mishit, vowing to be wide awake next time! Lohmann, of course, was the greatest of all medium-pace bowlers. There was intellect in his work, not mere cunning. A Yorkshire cricketer once told me that even when Lohmann was standing a drink he was all the time studying what sort of a batsman you were.

Parkin, with ever so little of Lohmann's ability to pursue a sustained plan of pace and break variation, would almost be as successful as the Surrey bowler himself was, especially in these days, with so many unwary, inexperienced batsmen about, a little overstrung in the race for honours. And while there is much in the idea that regular appearances in county cricket might " expose " Parkin, the view must also be considered that big cricket has its lessons for an earnest bowler with Parkin's rare natural endowments.

CHAPTER XXII

WILLIAM GUNN

In any form of activity greatness is more than skill or immense accomplishment; its touchstone is not to be found even in a highly individual style. The quality of greatness, surely, is most evident when an artist or craftsman so sums up in his work the typical characteristics of his occupation that we readily speak of him as the apogee of his art or craft. Genius of the first order gives us a consummation of its particular study; it leaves, or seems to leave, no potentialities wasting through lack of cultivation. That is why great men may be said to end, rather than to begin, epochs. William Gunn's work had this crowning glory. Nobody has succeeded him though his forerunners were many. He was the last of the " classical " batsmen.

The marks of that so-called " classical " period of batsmanship were forward play and a gracefulness that can without any misuse of language be called lyrical. Such a batsmanship is no longer with us, for the reason that modern bowling does not encourage it. To-day batsmanship is audacious, it is brilliant, it is challenging, it is versatile. You may call it all these things, but, taken in the lump, you cannot call it graceful. If Hobbs drives a short ball pitching on the off-side, as often enough he prefers to do, past mid-on, instead of forcing it past cover, the stroke moves you to surprise before it moves you to admiration. The sensations are not those which were awakened by Gunn's batting, nor by the typical batsman of his day. It was a different crowd psychologically that watched cricket in Gunn's days—a more tranquil crowd, one that lived in a world of less pace and changefulness than ours. One stresses the distinction the better to understand Gunn's manner, and the great hold he had on the cricket-lovers of his age. You will find on every pavilion in the country to-day men who speak of Gunn's batting as musicians speak of Mozart. His was the batting of felicity. It was content with sheer grace. You could watch it quite oblivious of the utilitarian consideration of whether runs were coming, and coming with match-winning speed. Often, in fact, Gunn gave the impression that he had fallen so completely in love with doing a beautiful thing for its own sake that the matter of his team's interests for the moment escaped him. Gunn was just as fascinating to watch in the nets as " in the middle." Even when the match was " fizzing out " into a draw the crowd would stay on just to look at him.

Gunn summed up the batsmanship of the 'eighties and 'nineties so completely that if nothing was left to us of the game's history during that period save the recollection of his art, we could re-construct it comprehensively enough from an examination of that art. His easeful forward style, at any rate, would

WILLIAM GUNN

tell us a good deal of the sort of bowling he had to meet. Graceful batsmanship depends on graceful bowling. Let a batsman be in doubt as to the length or direction of a delivery, and the precision of his cricket must suffer—and precision is three parts of good style. And it is only too true that the characteristic of modern bowling—especially since the googly came in—is unsteadiness of pitch, length, and spin. Forward play, as the " classical " batsmen employed it, is too great a speculation against bowling which is not immaculate in length and not fairly direct in spin. The batsman must have the ball on the ground with the secret of its break revealed before he can lunge at it, after the Gunn manner, with safety. " Classical " forward play was positively encouraged by bowlers of the Attewell and Shaw school. They used all their great arts towards the end of tempting you to lunge forward too far. In fact, the difference between modern bowling and the bowling of Gunn's period is that to-day bowlers seek to force you back to the wicket, while yesterday they sought to drag you out over the crease. And, of course, a man playing forward is prettier to watch than a man playing back.

Gunn, then, played cricket at a time when bowling favoured the style of batsmanship which we have all agreed to call " classical." He came just as Grace's superb lessons in the orthodox were in full circulation. Moreover, nature endowed him with great height and looseness of limb, and with these physical attributes he could exploit Grace's first principles unhindered by any of the impediments of bone and flesh which so often got in the master's way. There was also in Gunn's favour the fact that for the bulk of his batting he had the perfect wickets of Trent Bridge. In short, it would seem that there was a very conspiracy of circumstances towards the end of fashioning Gunn into the exemplar of the batsmanship of his time.

Old cricketers will tell you how proudly Gunn carried himself,—tall and as upright as any man of Hambledon. His height was 6 feet 3 inches, and he was built in proportion. He had all the strokes which Grace taught—all of them scrupulously scientific. But his personal presence and method put a bloom on the orthodox. The fastest bowling, even on a bumpy pitch, left him unruffled. The mechanism of his strokes was so precise that his strongest drive sent the ball along the grass. If he did hit to the on-side there was no suspicion of a " pull " in the stroke. The one doubtful hit in his repertory was a risky slash cut made at the pitch of a good length ball on the off. The ball went over cover-point's head, and gave the field some hope. Ranjitsinhji thought Gunn used this hit simply to keep the fieldsman's spirit from dying out altogether. Grace described Gunn in 1899, as " beyond all doubt one of the greatest professional batsmen England has seen." This is high praise, especially if we remember that Gunn had to stand a day-to-day comparison with Arthur Shrewsbury, his colleague in many a famous partnership.

CHAPTER XXIII

ALEC WATSON

1880 AND 1920—A CONTRAST

WATSON'S best period happened some thirty years years ago, and since then the conditions under which cricket is played have changed so much as to make rather futile the question which will inevitably spring up to-day—" Would Watson have been a successful bowler now ? "

That he bowled at batsmen like Grace, W. W. Read, Scotton, Shrewsbury, A. G. Steel, and Gunn, and against the straightest bats ever seen on the cricket field, could take his 100 wickets in a season at a cost of some twelve runs each, are facts which will, of course, command vast respect. But while we moderns are bound to honour the great bowlers of old, we are yet left free to argue that the job of getting men out must have been considerably easier on the fairly rough grounds of the eighties than it is in any summer in our age of marl and heavy rollers. Look into the old chronicles of the game, and you may read of the crowd at Lord's rising as a man to cheer " W. G." for stopping four " shooters " in an over from a fast bowler. What would happen on a modern cricket field if a batsman ran into four shooters in an afternoon? Would he not be totally overcome by the phenomenon and consider it a matter demanding scientific inquiry? There is a myth about Watson to the effect that he could bowl a " shooter " whenever he wanted. By what species of spin he managed the trick we are not told. Topspin, applied to a medium paced ball, even if it is bowled with a low flight from the bowler's arm, simply causes the ball to " nip " from the ground. There must, however, be an upward trajectory after the ball has hit the ground—unless it is made to " skid " by the condition of the wicket. We have many bowlers nowadays who can put top spin on a ball, but it is in the power of no man to send down a shooter at will, on a pitch which has a prepared cushion of grass.

But no admirer of Watson will want to make too much capital out of his " shooter." A crude ball at the best, it does not overcome the batsman so much by skill as by surprise. And the really fine point about Watson's bowling, as indeed it was the fine point about the bowling of all the " old masters," was that it challenged the batsman's mettle in the light of open day, with " skill for skill " the battle cry. The old bowlers were not " mystery bowlers." They did not get their men out simply by " taking them unawares." We might put down the old bowler's faith in these words: " I know your batting points; you know my bowling points. You've nothing up your sleeves, no more have I. Yet I'll beat you ! "

ALEC WATSON

When we take a glance at the modern slow-to-medium paced bowler's technique, and compare it with the technique of a cricketer like Watson, it is like looking from a music score by Stravinsky to one by Haydn. The one depends on its complications—one might even say its chromatic complications—a swerve, " googly," and variation in pace and flight; the other is content with sturdy diatonics—a good mechanical length and an off-break as obvious as the nose on your face. Even allowing for the difference between the wickets of Watson's day and those of our own, we cannot hold back astonishment that the old bowlers should have gone so far on capital so slender. How striking an idea of their mastery may we get if we will look at the subject this way: Watson bowled a ball just under medium pace and now and then used the conventional off-break. This delivery is not exactly fashionable in county cricket now, save on sticky wickets, and Cook of Lancashire bowls it better than anybody else, though not quite as subtly as Haigh and J. T. Hearne bowled it a few years ago. The deadliness of the off-break must have been greater to batsmen who did not cover the wickets with the pads in the wholesale way familiar to us.

Again, modern mastery over on-side play, with the pull and hook stroke brought to a Hendren's perfection, has also developed something like a specific for the off-break. The dangerous ball for the modern batsman is that which pitches on his leg-stump and swings across to the off; he must play it, the pads are no use here. Barnes was a genius with this delivery,

A CRICKETER'S BOOK

and when he exploited it even a Trumper, with *his* quick feet, was at a loss.

We can see, then, that the technique of batting has so changed since Watson's period that now the deadliest bowler is he whose best ball is in total contrast to Watson's best ball. Plainly, we cannot indulge in comparisons between the old bowling and the new; there is no means at hand whereby to equate our problem. All we can say is that Watson gave almost as much trouble to the great batsmen of the 'eighties as Barnes has done in our own time.

CHAPTER XXIV

M. A. NOBLE

THE general law which divides human mentality into two contrasted types,—making of us Liberals and Conservatives in politics, classicists and romancists in the arts and literature, Platonists and Aristoteleans in philosophy—would seem to operate even in our sports and pastimes. In cricket, at any rate, we have our Frys and our Ranjis, our Trumpers and our Nobles. M. A. Noble was in the classic school through and through, and that much can be said without contradicting the view that also he was definitely a player of to-day. For it is possible to be classic without being pedantic. Noble's style scrupulously observed all the principles which long experience has sanctioned, but with him these principles had, so to speak, developed naturally, and the ease with which he was able to adapt them, especially in his batting, to every change in the technique of the game, was a striking justification of their undiminishing utility.

As a bowler he was far enough advanced to cultivate the swerve, but even here he never forgot the time-honoured axiom about good length being the basis of good bowling. Too many of our "swervers" can only bring off their effects by over-pitching, and

A CRICKETER'S BOOK

indeed the very conditions which are required to induce the swerve render it difficult not to over-pitch. Before a ball will curl, obviously it must be in the air for a longish time, and take an uncommonly spacious curve in its flight. The trouble, therefore, is to swerve without presenting the batsman with the full toss or half-volley which can so easily be hit to the boundary. Noble solved the problem like the thoughtful student he was. He got the necessary addition to his curve in the air at his end of the pitch—not at the batsman's. This he managed by going down rather low on his right knee in the act of delivery, and by releasing the ball from the hand farther back in the swing over than is usual. The ball thus was impelled from a conveniently low altitude, and as a consequence, the upward trajectory was a little higher than the average bowler's, and so the ball gained the extra air in which to lose its spin—and this must happen before the swerve will take effect—all of which operations happened well away from the batsman's reach. His swerve was done so subtly that the batsman hardly saw it at all, for it was less a curve in from the right or the left than a vertical swerve. There was perhaps a slight swing from leg, but the chief danger came from the ball that dropped suddenly down just when it appeared certain to be a delightful half-volley. There was, however, nothing sensational in Noble's swerve; even a purist like Alfred Shaw might have cultivated it had he played the game to-day. As has been said, Noble always tried to keep his length classically correct.

M. A. NOBLE

He also had the conventional off-break of the fast medium bowler. But, first and last, it was his generalship that gave the quality to his bowling which made it difficult on all wickets. He was a master of deceptive flight, as, indeed, most great Australian bowlers invariably are. They need to be, too, playing as they do in a country where the hard, fast grounds so often make break almost impossible.

Noble's batting was in all its details quite classical; here no notably modern characteristic entered at all. His play did not fire the imagination of the crowd, like Trumper's; rather, it compelled admiration. There was thoughtfulness in his very stance at the wicket, and every action pointed to a deliberate and studiously cultivated method.

The art of Trumper is like the art in a bird's flight, an art that knows not how wonderful it is. With Noble there was always a sense of effort; we did not feel, as we did with Trumper, that batting was for him a superb dissipation, a spontaneous spreading of fine feathers. He gave us the impression, always, that there was some difficult obstacle in the attack to be overcome only by hard work and untiring determination. His was the skill that comes not exactly "after the manner born," but through diligently scorning delights and living laborious days. He played back to an extent uncommon among Australians. But it was back play of an extremely graceful and polished kind. He did not dab at the ball, bringing the bat from just behind the right leg with a cramped wrist action, as some batsmen do.

A CRICKETER'S BOOK

His bat, even in his very late defensive strokes, came down from above with a full swing; it was as free and as rhythmic as a forward shot. He combined caution with enterprise in a way that is typical of the average Australian cricketer. In his brilliant moments his off-drive was worth a day's walk to see.

P. F. Warner has described Noble as the wisest of all Australian captains, and though this is high praise, remembering Giffen and Darling, it must come very near the truth. On the field he was the picture of concentration. His temperament inclined him naturally towards the more scientific aspects of the game, and he usually wore the expression of a mathematician tussling with a stiff proposition. He played the game for all he was worth—as though, indeed, a kingdom depended on it. It will be best to remember him as a long-limbed and tense-featured giant standing abstractedly at point between the overs (where, by the way, he was one of the finest fielders of them all) knitting his brows and letting the whole world go by, save the particular scene of the moment,—the warm sun and the grass, the silently moving men in white, and the dire necessity of another wicket before lunch.

CHAPTER XXV

THE CRICKETER AS ARTIST

(August 1920)

WE are supposed to be well on the way towards decadence in an art as soon as we allow the parts to fascinate us rather more than the whole—when, for instance, a Debussy so falls in love with the attractiveness of his whole-tone scale harmonies that he neglects the main job of music, which is the expression of some sort of emotion. But decadent or no, it is only human to find great joy in a new technical dodge for its own sake. A man may decide to buy a cycle, meaning really to save money in railway fares from and to the city; none the less, the day the machine arrives he will take the thing out and ride it to nowhere in particular, simply exulting in a new toy. Probably he will also take it to pieces and lose a few important screws and things—out of what is at the bottom the artist's preoccupation with the way of doing things simply for the fascination of that way. This love of technique for technique's sake is a characteristic in English cricket to-day,—perhaps more than it has ever been before. The parts of cricket—bowling, batting and fielding—are now reaching an almost over-developed stage. In the beginning, we can imagine, twenty-two men met on a field, took sides, and had no other interest in cricket than to win the match. No matter how " old Lumpy " bowled " Nutty " out—grub or full toss—the great point was that he *was* out. And the lucky snick past slip looked just as well on the score-sheet as the neatest of cuts. In its earliest period, the parts of cricket were too crudely organized to invite specialism and all those distractions which specialism can easily cultivate to take a cricketer's attention from the job in hand—that of beating the other men. Played on a village green, rudely if lovingly, one could say of cricket, borrowing from Kipling, that " the game was more than the player of the game." Nothing but the lust for conquest and contest here—no wire-drawn appreciation of the fine shades; simply the wigs on the green and our team against the world.

There is a different viewpoint from this among cricketers now, and, indeed, among watchers of cricket. Who cares about the tussle for championship points if a Ranji be glancing to leg? Even the man who wants Surrey to get beaten cannot find it in his heart to complain if Hobbs scores a hundred. And what modern bowler that has felt the joy which comes of breaking a ball from the off with a leg-break action can resist the temptation of bowling his " googly " in season and out—aye, even if he knows that a good straight length ball would get his man out quicker? A summer or two ago the writer was coaching little boys at a public school. They chafed at having to pass through a course of conventional

THE CRICKETER AS ARTIST

bowling. "We'd rather get wickets with breaks and swerves than the straight stuff that the old 'uns used to bowl"—that was their view of the matter at the bottom. And only the other day, a great batsman in one of our counties, when he was bowled trying to hook an off-ball, explained his failure in these words: "Well, you simply can't go on hitting off balls past mid-off. Any fool is able to do that. One gets tired of doing things in the easiest way." The divine discontent of the artist, this, surely. Who that has a soul at all, be he bricklayer or maker of sonnets, is happy just moving along the lines of least resistance? Had Ranjitsinhji been content with fat scores made in the fashionable way, he could easily have gone on hitting balls from the middle stump straight to long on. But he was ever an artist, "tired of doing things in the easiest way,"—ever seeking to widen the scope of his craft, experimenting, creating obstacles for the sheer fun of overcoming them.

Was ever cricket so well off in the so-called classical days for artists, especially artist-bowlers, as the game has been these last few years, since the advent of B. J. T. Bosanquet and his disciples? Surely a man had to have an axe of partisanship to grind before he could rave for æsthetic reasons about the bowling of the Attewell school. A good length outside the off-stump all day—why, one of those new-fangled bowling machines would have been as interesting to watch. It was all right, of course, if you were watching the game for no other reason than to shout Nottinghamshire home, for undoubtedly Attewell did get his bags of wickets. But the man who goes to cricket solely to witness a contest is mistaking his game. Football can work off more combative energy in ten minutes than cricket in a summer. The summer game has, of course, its tight finishes—moments in which it is the team and not the individual that matters, moments in which one will cheer a full toss that gets a wicket and groan at the bowler whose fine off-break gets clouted for six. But these seasons of crisis come rarely in cricket. Normally the game is a spectacle as much as a contest. And because of that we must have our artist-cricketers—men who can get us interested in themselves, who can get interested in themselves, even though no finish of the game is in sight, and all is moving to the drawn match which bores the uninitiated onlooker. With Attewell bowling like an automaton and Scotton always taking the line of least resistance, the game needed to be won and lost. There was little, surely, in these cricketers but match-winning qualities. And, significantly enough, with the coming in recent summers of the great individualists like Fry, Ranji, Trumper, Bosanquet, the ancient lament about incompleted games has been heard less and less. Nobody worries about the draw—the uncompleted match which satisfies no lust for conquest, if an artist-batsman happens to be on view. Not long ago the most attractive side in the country was Sussex, with, of course, Ranji in the eleven. Yet they drew all, or nearly all, their matches.

Our grandfathers had, of course, their artist-

THE CRICKETER AS ARTIST

batsmen in no small numbers, and perhaps it is in bowling that modern cricket is infinitely more interesting * than cricket of yesterday to the onlooker who does not happen to be a partisan, but watches simply out of a love of the fine shades. Certain, anyhow, that our grandfathers never knew the "googly." When county groundsmen a few years ago started to make their pitches as perfect for batsmen as they knew how—mainly with an eye to a three days' gate—they probably broke the hearts of scores of average bowlers, who found that length and spin were not much use on those "shirt-front wickets." But the artist-bowler found only another occasion for joy in this new obstacle, and set himself to get over it. Then the "googly" came, the whole point of which is to deceive the batsman before the ball has pitched. What matter the state of the ground if you can beat your man in the air? And the perfect modern wicket saw also the development of the swerve—another device calculated to enable a bowler to snap his finger at the groundsman and his marl. Thus did bowling take on finer and finer points. To-day people actually go to a match to watch Parkin bowl—it is not only the batsman that is in the picture now! Mind you, they go not merely to watch Parkin bowl somebody out. Folk doubtless went to look at Alfred Shaw get wickets. It was the wickets going down that they liked; not bowling for its own sake. This last few summers

* "Interesting," I say—from the spectators' point of view; I do not mean that bowling now is better technically.

scores of cricketers have flocked to Lord's keen on Parkin's bowling and found it interesting whether or no he was getting wickets.

Specialism always makes the parts more and more interesting, and we have arrived at the time when cricket is in the hands of specialists. There is even a danger that the whole will suffer. You can get so much in love with the art of spinning the ball " the wrong way " that you begin to forget that without a good length a bowler is no match-winner. And as a long-hop is not even pretty to watch, you might even cease to be worth looking at. It is well, then, that in cricket, too, nature in the long run distributes fairly her Platonists and her Aristoteleans,—the men who walk by faith and the men who walk by reason. We have even yet such sturdy upholders of first principles as William Quaife and J. W. Hearne. But even Hearne bowls " googlies." There is no getting away from it—it is the hey-day of the cricketer artist, the man who simply will not do the job in the old-fashioned and easiest way.

PART II
THE TEST MATCHES 1921

NOTTINGHAM

LORD'S

LEEDS

MANCHESTER

OVAL

" Bravo, Cornstalks, ' whipt ' us,
  Fair and square! "

CHAPTER I

NOTTINGHAM

FIRST DAY, MAY 28th, 1921
(Scores at Close of Play.)

ENGLAND—First Innings.

D. J. Knight, c Carter, b Gregory	8
Holmes, b Macdonald	80
Tyldesley (E.), b Gregory	0
Hendren, b Gregory	0
J. W. H. T. Douglas, c Gregory, b Armstrong	11
Woolley, c Hendry, b Macdonald	20
V. W. C. Jupp, c Armstrong, b Macdonald	8
Rhodes, c Carter, b Gregory	19
Strudwick, c Collins, b Gregory	0
Howell, not out	0
Richmond, c and b Gregory	4
Extras	12
Total	112

AUSTRALIA—First Innings.

W. Bardsley, lbw. b Woolley	66
H. L. Collins, lbw, b Richmond	17
C. G. Macartney, lbw, b Douglas	20
J. M. Taylor, c Jupp, b Douglas	4
W. W. Armstrong, b Jupp	11
J. M. Gregory, lbw, b Richmond	14
C. E. Pellew, not out	21
H. Carter, not out	8
Extras	11
Total (6 wickets)	167

T. J. E. Andrews, H. L. Hendry, and E. A. Macdonald to bat.

A CRICKETER'S BOOK

The scoring card provides a fair anodyne for the pains that English cricket suffered at Trent Bridge on Saturday. On paper, in nice statistics, the truth is hidden. On paper, indeed, it might even seem that England has had but little the worse of the day's play and that an English victory in the end is not impossible. Would that one who watched the actual cricket could think these things—to soothe the memory of an evil day. English batsmanship in the morning was rubbed in the mire by Gregory and Macdonald; rarely indeed can Test match batsmen have been so completely reduced to littleness. Then, in the afternoon, Bardsley and Macartney played with England's bowling for all the world as though it were schoolboy's stuff.

The writer is unable even now—when the noise and passion of the day are gone—to explain the downfall of six Australian batsmen. Our bowlers looked feebleness itself after the fury of Gregory and Macdonald. One got the idea that the Australians were now indulging an easy view of affairs; four of them walked into their wickets to fall victims to obvious l.b.w. traps. Gifts from the gods were these wickets to England's bowlers. Taylor was brilliantly caught. Only one Australian batsman, in fact, was completely beaten and bowled, and he the mighty Armstrong. The others all faced the English attack confidently, and then unaccountably discovered themselves walking to the pavilion. The Australian innings passed its ways in peace where England's had been abominably scourged. The Australian batsmen had moments

NOTTINGHAM

of calm; England's batsmen found naught but travail and a desolate view.

The day's cricket began under a sky of fitting gloom. It was easy just now to imagine Trent Bridge some blasted heath with witches about making a sinister brew. A brave cheer from the multitude when Holmes and Knight came in to bat. Yet none of us quite liked the air of masterful confidence which the Australians had suggested as they went into the field—throwing negligent catches they were, and plainly making urbane conversation. And less did we like the way the Australians put aside these amenities. As Gregory got himself ready to attack not a man of them but looked grim and pitiless.

The prelude to the English innings was in the wrong key—it suited a merry tune. Knight scored a single from Gregory's second ball and then Holmes drove the first ball the fast bowler hurled at him to the off boundary and glanced the fourth to the leg boundary. The crowd buzzed out large appreciation; the noise ran round and the sound of it had a quite visual appeal. The batsmen played confidently enough at the beginning. Knight was stylish, and the flavour of the public school was about him. As he faced Macdonald and Gregory one thought of Newbolt's poem about the bumping pitch and the hush in the Close. But at the other end was Holmes, set to a determination that marked his face with lines of pain. What conflict these Australians bring to the game with a beautiful name! What an ordeal by battle they make of cricket!

The fate motif of England's innings sounded for the first time in Gregory's third over. Knight flashed his bat at a ball wide to the off side. He just snicked it. Carter caught the ball while the slips split the heavens with a jubilant appeal. Ernest Tyldesley was in next, and as he walked to the wicket his face was eager but composed. His very first ball defeated him. It came through the air at an appalling velocity. It pitched on the off wicket. Tyldesley brought down his bat hard and desperate. He only half stopped the deadly pace and the ball rolled to the leg stump and removed the bail. Tyldesley walked away disconsolate. Gregory's next delivery almost bowled Hendren. The next ball was good but harmless, and then Gregory bowled the most formidable ball I have seen in cricket for ages. It had lightning pace; it pitched outside the wicket and whipped back to knock Hendren's off stump flying. Poor Hendren's face, as he witnessed the coming of this fearsome ball, was all comical amazement. His mouth made Giotto's beautifully rounded letter " O."

Thus the score board now declared to a consternated crowd that England was a beggarly eighteen for three wickets. Two batsmen out for "ducks." One recollected a day at Lord's years ago when Hopkins dismissed Ranji and Fry for none. But in those days, England had her Jacksons and MacLarens to lean upon. Now, alas, master batsmen were absent. Holmes and Douglas toiled by the sweat of the brow in succour of the English side. Rain delayed play

NOTTINGHAM

for a period and prolonged the tension insufferably. Thirty-seven minutes dragged by before Australia thrust another hot iron on the struggling body of English cricket. With the score 38 for three Armstrong bowled instead of Macdonald. He exploited leg-breaks pitched outside the off stump, with six men on the off side,—one slip close to the batsman, two fairly deep, a backward point, a cover, and a mid-off. Three men were on the on side in front of the wicket. Armstrong pitched a tantalising length and plainly was seeking to entice Douglas into a hasty stroke. For a brief while Douglas was wary enough. But Armstrong continued to toss them well up to the bat and at last Douglas could deny himself no more. " What dost thou think I am " we could imagine him saying, like Meleander in Ford's play, " that thou should'st fiddle so much upon my patience?" Douglas went after Armstrong's eleventh ball, which dropped far to the off side, and he tried to hit but merely skied an easy catch. The stroke must have been the ghastliest ever made in Test cricket by a responsible batsman.

Woolley and Holmes, by immense toughness of spirit, now made the longest stand of the English innings. They actually scored thirty-four runs without losing their wickets. Woolley even in this bodeful hour was graceful and seemingly negligent. He made at least two sweet off drives. Armstrong bowled three overs only, rolling up to the wicket like some sea captain in a heavy swell, and had one wicket for no runs. After lunch the Australian fast

A CRICKETER'S BOOK

bowlers controlled the attack and England went down to ruin with hardly a kick.

Holmes was sixth out at 78 after an hour and a half's noble martyrdom. It was an innings full of the Yorkshire touch—courageous and skilful. England's last five wickets fell in the making of 35 runs. The side was overthrown wicket by wicket in this sequence:—

1	2	3	4	5	6	7	8	9	10
18	18	18	43	77	78	101	107	108	112

Gregory bowled unchanged, and Macdonald rested for three overs only. Better fast bowling has never been witnessed on English cricket fields since the days of Brearley and Knox. The wicket was good, its pace quite easy, yet these bowlers sent wickets spinning and broke the ball back with incredible venom. Macdonald also bowled a beautiful swinger now and again. Both men spared themselves not a jot of nerve and muscle. They were just demoniac. A magnificent field backed them up. Not a catch was missed, and the pace of the outfielders was fast indeed. Pellew is a sheer glory of speed and precision on the boundary.

During the English innings some talk was heard on the ground about a sporting wicket,—the Australian bowling had possessed such a vicious bite from the turf. But it was plain to everybody as soon as Howell and Douglas bowled that the pitch had no life, that it was a batsman's wicket. While Gregory and Macdonald bowled, the ground might have been

NOTTINGHAM

made of bone, with such speed and bounce did the ball come in. While England's bowlers laboured, the pitch might have been a hearthrug, so heavily and spiritlessly did the ball behave. Howell, after Gregory and Macdonald, was as a fair medium pace bowler. You could see him all the way, coming more or less straight through with never a break back to amaze the batsmen. Macartney batted audaciously and the cricket was brilliant while he lasted. Bardsley had periods of elegance but longer periods of mere prosiness. Collins lived up to the notion that he is the Martin Tupper of batsmen. Pellew attacked the bowling, and while he is undefeated England is in grave danger.

Douglas managed his bowling rather unimaginatively. With the Australians' total 29 for none, he allowed Richmond to bowl in his place with Howell. At 63 he went on again and rested Howell. These were the only bowling changes until the Australian score read 112 for three wickets. At 114, Woolley bowled, and two runs later Jupp. Douglas did not ask Rhodes to bowl at all. England's fielding was, on the whole, admirable. There was a crowd of some 20,000, and on the pavilion one saw many an old master of cricket—Warner, Spooner, Foster, Jessop—all cultivating an amount of dubiety. Armstrong left Mailey out of his side for this match, a clear indication that the wicket was easy.

A CRICKETER'S BOOK

SECOND AND LAST DAY, MONDAY, MAY 30, 1921.
(Final Scores.)

ENGLAND.

First Innings.		Second Innings.	
D. J. Knight, c Carter, b Gregory	8	run out	88
Holmes, b Macdonald	30	c Taylor, b Macdonald	8
Tyldesley (E.), b Gregory	0	b Gregory	7
Hendren, b Gregory	0	b Macdonald	7
J. W. H. T. Douglas, c Gregory, b Armstrong	11	c Hendry, b Macdonald	13
Woolley, c Hendry, b Macdonald	20	c Carter, b Hendry	34
V. W. C. Jupp, c Armstrong, b Macdonald	8	c Pellew, b Gregory	15
Rhodes, c Carter, b Gregory	19	c Carter, b Macdonald	10
Strudwick, c Collins, b Gregory	0	b Hendry	0
Howell, not out	0	not out	4
Richmond, c and b Gregory	4	b Macdonald	2
Extras	12	Extras	9
Total	112	Total	147

AUSTRALIA.

First Innings.		Second Innings.	
W. Bardsley, lbw, b Woolley	66	not out	8
H. L. Collins, lbw, b Richmond	17		
C. G. Macartney, lbw, b Douglas	20	not out	22
J. M. Taylor, c Jupp, b Douglas	4		
W. W. Armstrong, b Jupp	11		
J. M. Gregory, lbw, b Richmond	14		
C. E. Pellew, c and b Rhodes	25		
H. Carter, b Woolley	33		
T. J. E. Andrews, c and b Rhodes	6		
H. L. Hendry, not out	12		
E. A. Macdonald, c Knight, b Woolley	10		
Extras	14		
Total	232	Total (for 0 wkts.)	30

NOTTINGHAM

Australian Bowling—First Innings.

	O.	M.	R.	W.		O.	M.	R.	W.
Gregory	19	5	58	6	Armstrong	8	3	0	1
Macdonald	15	5	42	3					

Second Innings.

Gregory	22	8	45	2	Armstrong	27	10	33	0
Macdonald	22.4	10	82	5	Hendry	9	1	18	2
Macartney	5	2	10	0					

England Bowling—First Innings.

	O.	M.	R.	W.		O.	M.	R.	W.
Howell	9	3	22	0	Woolley	22	8	46	3
Douglas	13	2	84	2	Jupp	5	0	14	1
Richmond	16	3	69	2	Rhodes	13	3	33	2

Second Innings.

Jupp	8.1	0	18	0	Richmond	8	0	17	0

This match was well lost on Saturday morning—England never looked up after that woeful first half-hour before lunch, and to-day the Australians drove home the advantage relentlessly. England's batsmen did little that was handsome, and so fortune looked the other way. There was a bare chance of a fight by Tyldesley and Knight in the afternoon, but cruel luck frustrated it. Tyldesley had settled down to confident cricket when a ball from Gregory rose sharply, and after striking him in the face fell on the wicket. A misunderstanding with Hendren ran out Knight just as he looked in a happy mood—good for a big innings.

These accidents must, of course, be stressed in fairness to the England eleven. Little enough, though, can one find wherewith to explain away this latest defeat, save terms indicative of cricket in a class well below Australian quality. To-day the pitch gave a slight aid to Armstrong's bowlers, but for no considerable period. Apart from Knight, only Woolley consistently held himself like a Test match batsman. There is no getting away from the truth—Australian cricket, especially the bowling and fielding, is better than ours.

Heavy rain fell at dawn, and though the day turned fine after breakfast the question at eleven o'clock was how the pitch would behave. For an hour at least the turf might respond quite dully to spin and bite sharply after lunch. The game for England was to get the Australians out quickly and seek to cancel the enemy's advantage before the bowlers discovered a convenient wicket. How the way of the turf lay at the outset one could deduce from Douglas's choice of England's bowlers when the match was resumed. He selected Woolley and Rhodes. The crowd cheered—ironically, it seemed —Douglas's belated sanction for the popular notion that Rhodes is even yet a bowler. And Rhodes turned the occasion, now that he was at last in contrast with Woolley, and vastly to his advantage. Even Douglas, after this morning's cricket, must admit that Woolley is not in the same class as a left-hand slow bowler with Rhodes.

Both Woolley and Rhodes had two wickets this morning at much the same cost. But Woolley hardly ever looked difficult, while all the time Rhodes did. When Pellew was baffled by Rhodes's hanging slow ball the Australian tail was in, yet Woolley continued

NOTTINGHAM

to bowl mainly outside the off stump for all the world as though great men at the cover-drive were batting. He wasted a man in the slips for an hour the while Carter scraped valuable runs from strokes to leg which might have been caught had more than a solitary scout been there. Woolley did not bowl to a slips trap; mainly he exploited the left-hander's old trick —the ball that goes with the arm. And surely a successful exploitation of this trick depends on at least two leg-side fieldsmen. Almost an hour passed away this morning before the field was arranged appropriately on the on-side for Woolley.

The Australian innings finished at a quarter-past twelve. Carter was allowed to make 33 precious runs. Rhodes was unlucky not to get him out quite early in the morning. The English fielding had none of the Australian dash and tact. It was competent, but too many men moved heavily, too many saw a hit flash by them the while they rather resembled somebody in one of Sir F. C. Gould's studies in still life. England needs keen youth in large quantities just now.

Against Australia's pull of 120, England went in again an hour before lunch. Knight and Holmes regarded Gregory and Macdonald dubiously at the outset. But the pitch was too heavy just now for fast bowling. After pounding two overs, Gregory was rested, and Macartney bowled. Macartney adapted himself to the new conditions skilfully. He slackened pace and explointed a break-back. Holmes, playing the break correctly enough, but not going through with his strokes, pushed one of these breakbacks into the air on the on-side, and so fell into a simple trap.

Ernest Tyldesley passed through an eternity of maiden overs before lunch, with the spectre of another nought in front of him; but just on lunch time he scored one, and so could take sustenance in peace. For half an hour after the interval England moved along a smooth way. Knight used his bat with the artist's grace, and Tyldesley was plainly beginning to see the ball fine and large against the white screen. The wicket nipped but rarely. Then, as the crowd sat as quiet as a mouse, England ran into disaster. Tyldesley was dismissed in a way wellnigh heart-breaking. Gregory pitched a fast ball woefully short, and it shot viciously into Tyldesley's face. He sought to hook it but was not quick enough. The ball struck him on the right jaw, and while he held breath he fell to the grass like a stone. The Australian fieldsmen dashed to the wicket to succour him. Gestures were made to the pavilion. Then Tyldesley lifted himself up and was taken from the field. The crowd sighed relief that after all no great accident had happened, but relief turned to stupefaction when the score board announced that Tyldesley was out. Seemingly the bumping ball had found a way to Tyldesley's wicket after half-stunning him. Never has a cricketer been so churlishly handled by fortune in the great event of his life. The crowd vented its mortification by barracking Gregory whenever he bowled a short ball.

NOTTINGHAM

Hendren, the next man in, patted the turf half-way down the wicket—like the humorist he is. The crowd now went dumb again—needing, no doubt, some recovery of breath. And rather before a proper control of respiratory organs had been achieved, the blow fell on England which seemingly knocked her flat. Knight and Hendren fell into confusion between the wickets and Knight was run out. The crowd in an understandable chagrin sought for somebody to blame. But neither Knight nor Hendren obviously invited censure—bad luck is the convenient term to use in explanation of this mistake. Knight in his brave innings conducted himself like a Test match man all the time. He forced the fast bowling in front of the wicket boldly. His innings lasted an hour and three-quarters and staked firmly his claim to a place in England's next Test match side.

Woolley batted capitally, too—he had a firm back-stroke for Gregory's short balls, and he played it straight and never behind the back leg. None of the other batsmen were resolute enough for the Australian bowlers: there was too much speculative half-cock batsmanship about. England by hook or crook must discover some forcing cricketer to go in late. Fender might be given another chance. The Australian fielding was superb to the end. Pellew on the boundary had the speed and grace of a deer, and there was hardly ever a hole at all through the slips.

CHAPTER II

LORD'S

FIRST DAY, JUNE 11. 1921.
(Score at Close of Play.)

ENGLAND—First Innings.

D. J. Knight, c Gregory, b Armstrong	7
Dipper, b Macdonald	11
Woolley, st Carter, b Mailey	95
Hendren, b Macdonald	0
J. W. H. T. Douglas, b Macdonald	84
A. J. Evans. b Macdonald	4
L. H. Tennyson, st Carter, b Mailey	5
N. Haig, c Carter, b Gregory	8
Parkin, b Mailey	0
Strudwick, c Macdonald, b Mailey	8
Durston, not out	6
Extras	14
Total	187

AUSTRALIANS—First Innings.

W. Bardsley, not out	88
T. J. E. Andrews, c Strudwick, b Durston	9
C. G. Macartney, c Strudwick, b Durston	31
C. E. Pellew, b Haig	43
J. M. Taylor, not out	15
Extras	5
Total (for three wickets)	191

W. W. Armstrong, J. M. Gregory, H. L. Hendry, H. Carter, A. A. Mailey, and E. A. Macdonald to bat.

There is " damnable iteration " about these Test matches. On Saturday at Lord's we had the sad tale of Trent Bridge all over again. England was routed on a perfect wicket for 187, after some three hours and a half of travail, and then the Australians turned our bowlers into batsmen's playthings, and at the day's close had scored 191 for three wickets by cricket whose main note was cock-a-hoop audacity. Saturday's tale, indeed, is even more pitiable than the tale of Trent Bridge, where England's batsmen were at least overthrown by superlative bowling. But this time, Gregory was not himself; he had fallen away vilely since the last action. His pace was merely medium; it had bated, dwindled. Macdonald was the one authentic Test match bowler in the Australian XI. Yet our batsmen again faltered.

The first half-hour of the game saw Knight, Dipper, and Hendren overthrown for 25 runs. At Trent Bridge, England in much the same time, lost three wickets for 18. But then there was reason for the ruin—Gregory at Nottingham was a Spofforth come to youth again. The Australian attack on Saturday had simply day-to-day county efficiency in it. In the dreadful opening half-hour it may turn out that England lost this match, and it was through shockingly feeble, nerveless batsmanship. Knight went out of his way to follow a leg-break from Armstrong, which, as it had pitched outside the off stump, was breaking away harmlessly. And Knight by a ghastly stroke sent the ball into Gregory's hands in the slips. Dipper, who was beginning to shape confidently, produced a primitive mowing stroke which he must have learned in his native hamlet of Tewkesbury, and a good length ball from Macdonald beat the crooked bat. Hendren was out for nothing from the third ball he had sent him. It was a fast one, well up, and seemed to break in, but no uncommon venom was in it. Hendren simply did not play a straight stroke at it. What a piece of irony is this batsman's experience turning to! On most days in the summer he is living in a batsman's paradise at Lord's, piling up heavy hundreds. Then the Australians come— and he is starving for boundaries. How must his centuries made day-by-day against English counties mock him—he is a Barmecide at a feast.

When the score-board on Saturday announced England 25 for three wickets the crowd said "It's just tragic." But there was really nothing tragic in the cricket at all. Tragedy begins when something that is strong and fine suffers frustration. There was nothing fine and strong in England's cricket in that first half-hour, and consequently no sense of conflict or frustration. Nothing was there indeed but weakness and littleness. Never can an England eleven have dropped to so low a level of incompetent batsmanship as this latest England Eleven on Saturday morning.

Douglas and Woolley put an end to the stampede. From ten minutes past twelve till lunch at 1.30 did these two cricketers defend their wickets. The hour hung heavily about them, and even Woolley dared not venture boldly. The Australians, exultant and grim, sought to force quickly-gained advantages right home and so bring about a total eclipse of England. But Douglas and Woolley at least held straight bats and hung to their creases tenaciously. Perhaps they were fighting in the Fabian way too long. Many loose balls from Armstrong and Gregory they let pass unprofitably. Still, it was a boon to see even a passive resistance in the English ranks. From the moment Douglas joined Woolley until the interval, some 154 balls were bowled at them, and 48 runs came to England's aid without the loss of another wicket. Dour work and intolerable, surely, to Woolley's happy spirit.

After lunch both batsmen put the Australian bowling in the right light, and showed its mere competency to everybody. In little more than half an hour Woolley and Douglas scored 81 runs, and then Douglas strained fortune a little too severely and was bowled by Macdonald's slow ball. The stand by Woolley and Douglas produced 88 runs. It saved England from ignominy. No batsman but Douglas gave Woolley the faintest aid. Douglas was out at 108 and then six wickets fell for 79 runs, and of these Woolley made 51. The " experiments in new blood "—that is, Tennyson, Evans, and Haig—all bowed considerably under the weight of the occasion. Tennyson's efforts to drive Mailey in front of the wicket were wistful indeed. The form of Evans suggested that he would not only enjoy himself but be the source of enjoyment to others—in a country-house match. These tough Australians found easy game in him on Saturday. The fall of England's wickets tells the sad tale pretty completely:—

1	2	3	4	5	6	7	8	9	10
20	24	25	108	120	145	156	157	170	187

A CRICKETER'S BOOK

Nine batsmen compiled 44 between them! Woolley, in first wicket down and out last of all in a gallant striving for his century, batted for three hours and ten minutes and scored his 95 out of 167. It was a beautiful innings, and because of the circumstances in which it was fashioned, it was a sad innings. When sheer grace moves along ways that are inimical to it, pricking us with a sense of its frailty, we are at the source of pathos. On Saturday Woolley was always graceful, but how it did seem that the Australian bowlers baited him. One thought of the hunted stag. The true course of Woolley's exquisite art is a wayward and care-free course; on Saturday he had perforce to go heavily along a responsible way. All in all, thinking of the ruinous setting this innings was made in, it must be written down as a poem in batsmanship. Woolley drove heroically and gave one chance only, and that when he was hitting at everything in the eighties. Woolley's drives were invariably firm-footed, and seemingly nothing but arm-swing produced the great power of them. He very wisely chose for this stroke only balls pitching on or near the wicket. His body was thus kept well over the ball and the right foot close to the line of it (Woolley, of course, is a left-handed batsman). There was immense cleverness in his judgment whether a ball should be driven in front of the wicket or waited for a little longer and cut square on the rise from the pitch.

The Australian bowling was on the whole steady enough, but Macdonald alone looked dangerous. He

LORD'S

was faster than Gregory and plainly he is a more resourceful bowler than Gregory. If Gregory cannot work up his best pace—and he could not on Saturday—he has nothing of artifice to fall back upon. Macdonald's bowling has generalship in it; his length is varied according to the reach of a particular batsman, and his flight and pace vary too. Armstrong bowled eighteen overs, twelve of which were maidens, for nine runs and one wicket. As usual he exploited leg-breaks pitched on the wicket or slightly to the off side. One noticed G. L. Jessop in the crowd, and wondered how long Armstrong would have been permitted to bowl maiden overs to him. It is hard, indeed, to discover from the ring wherein Armstrong's leg-breaks are more " unhittable " than those of any other competent exploiter of this old-fashioned means of attack. The English batsmen played him safely enough on Saturday, but having got themselves into position for driving, seemed to lose heart at the last minute. Are our batsmen getting afraid of Armstrong because he is Australia's captain? When Armstrong was merely an ordinary member of an Australian side, batsmen did not hesitate to hit him. They were then as valiant as any Hercules in face of Armstrong. Is it that nowadays they have all come to " beware instinct ? " Will not the lion touch the true prince?

Australia's batting was, for an hour or so, just dazzling. In twenty-five minutes 51 runs were scored for Andrews's wicket—and he got out through sheer impatience. At the end of the first ten overs bowled by Douglas, Durston, and Parkin, the Australian score was 72. Douglas rested himself after sending down eighteen balls for 29 runs—including four boundaries. The Australians rounded the 100 mark in five minutes under the hour, and reached 150 in one hour and a half—this furious tempo in a Test match! Macartney was audacity in the flesh. Only Hobbs among living batsmen could have played his superb little innings of 81. His bat was a harlequin's wand. You could not follow all its flashings, curves, and thrusts. His foot-work was quick, and as occasion needed, took him far outside the crease, or back inside it to the wickets base,—yet the movements were so rapid that at the actual making of a stroke his stance was quite composed. Macartney cut late perkily and sweetly, cracking the ball on top with an almost flippant bat. He batted for but twenty-five minutes, and scored his 81 from twenty-two balls in this way:—2, 1, 4, 1, 0, 4, 0, 4, 1, 2, 0, 1, 0, 0, 0, 4, 0, 4, 0, 2, 1, 0.

Bardsley was in a classic mood, and his innings, though it had pace, had little apparent energy or effort. Here, at last, is a batsman who plainly has never heard of the "two-eyed stance." He plays forward more than Woolley, letting the right shoulder point in the direction of the stroke. Yet he is not inferior to Woolley in back play, and it is this mastery over both forward and back play that puts him well in front of Woolley as a left-handed batsman. Because of his fine forward method, Bardsley can score from fast good length bowling where Woolley

LORD'S

would need to wait for slightly short ones. Bardsley's innings is not done with yet, and may be left over for detailed discussion till it is. Pellew batted like a man on holiday. "This a Test match?" he seemed to say. "Now does it look like one, I ask you?"

Durston bowled with determination, and had life from the pitch, but Parkin was a shadow of the man who got Sussex out the other day—his length until the end of the afternoon fell on the short side. In the last over of the day he strove desperately to catch a hard and high return drive from Bardsley, but in vain. Still, it was good to see the essential spirit of the man flame out again. For the most part of the afternoon, though, it was a diminished Parkin that Lord's saw, not the gay incorrigible that Old Trafford knows. No maiden over was achieved by an England bowler until the score was 116. Later Parkin bowled a maiden and moved the multitude to applause. England's fielding was only moderate.

A CRICKETER'S BOOK

SECOND DAY, JUNE 13, 1921.
(Scores at Close of Play.)

ENGLAND.

First Innings.		Second Innings.	
D. J. Knight, c Gregory, b Armstrong	7	c Carter, b Gregory	1
Dipper, b Macdonald	11	b Macdonald	40
Woolley, st Carter, b Mailey	95	c Hendry, b Mailey	93
Hendren, b Macdonald	0	c Gregory, b Mailey	10
J. W. H. T. Douglas, b Macdonald	84	b Gregory	14
A. J. Evans, b Macdonald	4	lbw, b Macdonald	14
L. H. Tennyson, st Carter, b Mailey	5	not out	44
N. Haig, c Carter, b Gregory	8	b Macdonald	0
Parkin, b Mailey	0	c Pellew, b Macdonald	11
Strudwick, c Macdonald, b Mailey	8	not out	6
Durston, not out	6		
Extras	14	Extras	10
Total	187	Total (for 8 wkts.)	243

AUSTRALIANS—First Innings.

W. Bardsley, c Woolley, b Douglas	88
T. J. E. Andrews, c Strudwick, b Durston	9
C. G. Macartney, c Strudwick, b Durston	31
C. E. Pellew, b Haig	43
J. M. Taylor, lbw, b Douglas	36
W. W. Armstrong, b Durston	0
J. M. Gregory, c and b Parkin	52
E. L. Hendry, b Haig	5
H. Carter, b Durston	46
A. A. Mailey, c and b Parkin	5
E. A. Macdonald, not out	17
Extras	10
Total	342

If Macaulay's New Zealander had come upon Lord's at three o'clock to-day he might have imagined that England was winning. The vast crowd was in a frenzy of jubilation; the Australian fieldsmen ran helter-skelter all over the place. Gregory and Macdonald were out of action—they had been flogged to impotence. Armstrong wore a long face. For Dipper and Woolley were both setting the dreaded Australians at defiance by immensely resolute batsmanship. Well did it seem now that the tide of England's fortune had turned even in the darkest hour.

At 2.15 England had gone in again hopelessly behind, and Knight was out with a mere three runs scored—out from a wretched stroke. The Australians, sniffing yet more of ill tidings for England in the wind, bowled and fielded like demons. And the Gloucester man, Dipper, pale and gawky, with Woolley, all conceivable grace, changed for a while the game's course, and changed it totally. In an hour and a half these batsmen made 94 runs for England's second wicket. It was not merely that they scored the runs; the crowd howled delight because Australia's fast bowlers had at last been checked, nay, routed for the moment. This gallant stand may have a vast moral influence on the Test matches yet to be played. For it was demonstrated by Woolley and Dipper that Gregory and Macdonald are human enough and can be lustily hit. Dipper was bowled just as it seemed that he was seeing the ball as big as a football. He played strong and fearless cricket.

Yet Dipper, well though he conducted himself, was really out of the picture—he was, as it were, at the piano in a Kreisler valse. It was Woolley, Woolley all the way. What an innings he gave us—this tall man of Kent, as Nyren would have called him. Earlier in the day we all had thought that the highest excellence in left-handed batsmanship was touched by Bardsley. And Bardsley's work could not well have been bettered. The difference between his batsmanship and Woolley's was simply the difference between prose and poetry. The one charmed the intelligence, the other the æsthetic sensibility.

Woolley was at the wicket two hours and a half and scored 93 out of 162. No other cricketer, save Clement Hill, has come so near two hundreds in a Test match without getting one. Woolley's driving this afternoon was brilliant beyond words until he got himself out playing rather carelessly at an atrocious ball. He was master over the bowling all the time. He hit twelve fours. His off-drives had the finest power, yet they were seemingly made by the gentlest and most gracefully curving bat in the world. It was all cricket that touched the senses as Milton's " L'Allegro " touches them or as the " Little Night " music of Mozart. I have rarely seen batsmanship of such lightsome grace as this. The remaining English batting was ineffectual in comparison. Tennyson drove energetically at the day's close, but desperation, not mastery, was in it. The Australian bowling and fielding took on new life after Woolley was out. But we have had its limitations exposed to-day, and though the Ashes are hardly likely to come back to England this summer, the prospect of at least one victory to England is not quite as remote as it was on Saturday.

The sky was sullen earlier in the day when the game went on, and a chill wind passed over the field. A proper setting for the match the elements made. Would you have a Shakespeare send a Macbeth to discover witches in June sunshine? Let the scene suit the occasion, even at a game. This morning it was in the air that we all were assisting at the obsequies of English cricket, and so the grey clouds and the unhappy wind were meet for the hour. And never mind what your Ruskin has to say about the pathetic fallacy!

The English bowlers did deserve a little approving sunshine at the outset. Durston started the day with a superb maiden to Taylor, and then Douglas with his third ball, which swung away from the batsman at a perfect length, got Bardsley caught at slip. Whereupon Armstrong ambled to the wicket. He took a leg-stump guard and bent ponderously over the bat, which in his possession looks like a child's. He stopped four good balls from Douglas, and then used a back stroke to a fine break-back from Durston and saw his middle stump sent flying. Armstrong surveyed the wrecked wicket indifferently, even indulged in a broad grin at Strudwick, and went home to the pavilion, still ambling comfortably. The crowd now lifted up its spirit. There were, after all, bowlers in England. Alas! the best bowlers are bond-slaves to the field, and England's fielding now dwindled badly. Gregory, when he was eight, sent a slip catch to Evans. It was fast, and the fieldsman had to jump sideways to the right. He dropped the ball after getting his two hands to it, and the crowd made anguished noise. The Australian batting might easily have fallen to pieces at this point.

Taylor made the luckiest snick from Durston, and Gregory was missed again by Evans at 33. Nothing, indeed, came off for the English bowlers, whose energy and skill were far beyond their Saturday's showing. Taylor and Gregory added 88 for the sixth wicket, and Taylor then walked in front of his wicket to a straight ball. He is the one man in the Australian ranks whose cricket is sullied by what is bad in two-eyed stance influence.

The seventh Australian wicket lifted the score to 263, Hendry keeping Gregory company. Hendry batted like a man who has just learned the first principle of batsmanship, which is to keep a straight bat, and has learned no more than that. Scoring strokes had he none. He was at the wicket thirty-five minutes without opening his score, and permitted Haig to send him thirty balls for four runs only, and these made by one hit. Gregory did not dawdle, even if his batsmanship was stiff in the arm. He scored 52 out of 85 in seventy-five minutes from 66 balls. Still, with all Gregory's cubbish aggressiveness, Australia had nine wickets down for 289. Six wickets had fallen in the morning for 98. Imagine our consternation, then, that the last wicket should proceed to harry both the bowling and the fielding to the extent of 53 runs, all of them pressing heavily on England. During this rearguard action the English fielding was abominable; the ground work and returns slovenly enough for the village green. The Australian innings lasted four and a quarter hours, and left England 155 behind.

The bowling of Douglas, Durston, and Parkin deserved better rewards than came its way in this innings. Had the Australians fielded for England, neither Gregory nor Carter would have endured long. Parkin had a long and skilful spell and took two wickets for some thirty runs, and a catch was missed from him. He managed his length accurately and exploited a slowish leg-break cannily. Haig did good work with an off-break, and Durston was always bowling with all his heart. Slack fieldsmen were England's bugbear this morning.

The Australian batting after Bardsley lost his wicket was definitely moderate. But Bardsley gave us as skilful a piece of batsmanship as any left-hander since Clement Hill. For two hours and ten minutes he was on view, chaste all the time. In one point his cricket provided an object-lesson, which one trusts was not lost on the English batsmen. He played back perfectly straight, yet as he did so took advantage of the two-eyed stance opportunities for a full and quick sight of the ball. That is to say, he extracted what is good from the two-eyed stance and avoided the evil. Even when he turned his body almost square to the bowler, letting the forward shoulder swing round so that the vision of both eyes was not obstructed, none the less did he hold his bat in the pure upright. This he achieved by keeping his left shoulder (remember Bardsley is left-handed) close to the line of the ball and the right hand close to the left side. As the failing with the English batsmen in the lump on Saturday came from crooked strokes in back play it is fervently to be hoped that Bardsley's innings was studiously pondered by them and made a note of.

LORD'S

THIRD DAY, JUNE 14, 1921.

(Final Scores.)

ENGLAND.

First Innings.		Second Innings.	
D. J. Knight, c Gregory, b Armstrong	7	c Carter, b Gregory	1
Dipper, b Macdonald	11	b Macdonald	40
Woolley, st Carter, b Mailey	95	c Hendry, b Mailey	93
Hendren, b Macdonald	0	c Gregory, b Mailey	10
J. W. H. T. Douglas, b Macdonald	84	b Gregory	14
A. J. Evans, b Macdonald	4	lbw, b Macdonald	14
L. H. Tennyson, st Carter, b Mailey	5	not out	74
N. Haig, c Carter, b Gregory	8	b Macdonald	0
Parkin, b Mailey	0	c Pellew, b Macdonald	11
Strudwick, c Macdonald, b Mailey	8	b Gregory	12
Durston, not out	6	b Gregory	2
Extras	14	Extras	12
Total	187	Total	283

AUSTRALIANS.

First Innings.		Second Innings.	
W. Bardsley, c Woolley, b Douglas	88	not out	63
T. J. E. Andrews, st Strudwick, b Durston	9	lbw, b Parkin	49
C. G. Macartney, c Strudwick, b Durston	31	b Durston	8
C. E. Pellew, b Haig	43	not out	5
J. M. Taylor. lbw, b Douglas	36		
W. W. Armstrong, b Durston	0		
J. M. Gregory, c and b Parkin	52		
H. L. Hendry, b Haig	5		
H. Carter, b Durston	46		
E. A. Mailey, c and b Parkin	5		
E. A. Macdonald, not out	17		
Extras	10	Extras	6
Total	342	Total (for 2 wkts.)	131

A CRICKETER'S BOOK

Australian Bowling—First Innings.

	O.	M.	R.	W.		O.	M.	R.	W.
Gregory	16	1	51	1	Armstrong	18	12	9	1
Macdonald	20	2	58	4	Mailey	14.2	1	55	4

Second Innings.

	O.	M.	R.	W.		O.	M.	R.	W.
Gregory	26.2	4	76	4	Hendry	4	0	15	0
Macdonald	23	3	89	4	Mailey	25	4	72	2
Armstrong	12	6	19	0					

England Bowling—First Innings.

	O.	M.	R.	W.		O.	M.	R.	W.
Durston	24.1	2	102	4	Haig	20	4	61	2
Douglas	9	1	53	2	Woolley	11	2	44	0
Parkin	20	5	72	2					

Second Innings.

	O.	M.	R.	W.		O.	M.	R.	W.
Durston	9.3	0	84	1	Parkin	9	0	31	1
Douglas	6	0	23	0	Woolley	3	0	10	0
Haig	3	0	27	0					

England lost their match at Lord's well in time for lunch to-day. The Australians were asked to get 129 to win, thanks to big-hearted hitting by Tennyson at the day's outset. With the wicket still perfect nobody, of course, expected an Australian collapse. But everybody did look to Douglas for a fight with some gusto, even impudence, in it. A miracle, of course, was needed to bring home an English victory —some touch of inspiration, some drastic trafficking with fortune.

England had everything to gain and nothing to lose by a bold policy. And did Douglas play the gambler's last and often lucky throw? He did not. He proceeded to manage his bowlers just as he would have managed his own Essex county bowlers in a common, day-by-day match at Leyton. He went on

LORD'S

with Durston, and between them they bowled the sheerest routine stuff until the Australians had scored 40 in twelve overs. Then Douglas, working strictly to copy-book maxims, had a double change, Parkin bowling for himself and Haig bowling for Durston. By now both Andrews and Bardsley had been played in. Any chance of a fighting finish depended entirely on whether Parkin was in a match-winning mood. He was not asked to bowl until the Australians were well away to victory, and so could not exploit any mood of uncertainty, however slight, that conceivably might have been somewhere hidden under the faces of brass Bardsley and Andrews put on. As a fact, both batsmen began so badly that with Parkin at his best at them they might easily have got out.

Parkin, so it turned out, was in a merely competent vein. He did not suggest the match-winner. But Douglas did not know this at the outset of the Australian innings, and he ought certainly to have known that for a fighting finish there was no bowler in his team more likely than Parkin to run amuck, given the cue to do so straight away. No doubt there was no real chance of a close struggle on that splendid turf; still drastic generalship might have lessened the blow that fell on England. To permit batsmen with only 129 needed for victory to get three parts on the way without a change of bowling at all was dull-spirited indeed.

The English fielding was again poor; in fact, the team at the end very definitely had no stomach for the fight.

CHAPTER III

LEEDS

FIRST DAY, JULY 2nd, 1921.
(Scores at Close of Play.)

AUSTRALIANS—First Innings.

W. Bardsley, c Woolley, b Douglas	6
T. J. Andrews, c Woolley, b Douglas	19
C. G. Macartney, lbw, b Parkin	115
C. E. Pellew, c Hearne, b Woolley	52
J. M. Taylor, c Douglas, b Jupp	50
J. M. Gregory, b Parkin	1
H. L. Hendry, b Parkin	0
W. W. Armstrong, c Brown, b Douglas	77
H. Carter, b Jupp	84
E. A. Macdonald, not out	21
A. A. Mailey, c and b Parkin	6
Extras	26
Total	407

ENGLAND—First Innings.

Woolley, b Gregory	0
Hardinge, not out	11
Hearne, b Macdonald	7
Ducat, not out	8
Extra	1
Total (two wickets)	22

L. H. Tennyson, J. W. H. T. Douglas, V. W. C. Jupp, J. C. White, Hobbs, Brown and Parkin to bat.

The ancient story comes again—these Test matches would drive your Herodotus to play the parrot. On Saturday Australia's sovereignty persisted, and once more the heads of English cricketers are diminished.

LEEDS

Let some Lear of our game rail at Victory and say she will never come again. Armstrong, broad Achilles—but where is his heel?—may continue his deep chest laughs and cry " Excellent ! " This time fortune was good to him from the beginning. Australia had first innings on a fast and smooth turf, with the hot sunshine burning England's bowlers pitilessly. And Australia's batsmen prevailed, often by grace of that same good fortune, till the afternoon's fall, and then in a fading light England was compelled to face Gregory and Macdonald, and lost Woolley and Hearne for a mere score of runs.

But the story this time, after all, may give scope for some variation on the too familiar theme. England's trouble on Saturday most certainly did not come absolutely through her cricketers' lack of ability, measured with that of the Australians. Luck was plainly against us. Tennyson, the new captain, had his left hand split between thumb and first finger in the first hour of the game, and he was thus compelled to look on for the rest of the day. Late in the afternoon Hobbs was afflicted by an indisposition which made him helpless in the afternoon's last two hours.

And not content with frowning on England, Fortune must needs positively ogle Armstrong and his men. The Australian batsmen discovered a difficult English attack at the morning's outset, and did none too well with it for a while. And Macartney, Pellew, and Taylor only managed to put the game right for Australia after perilous escapades; all of them were

A CRICKETER'S BOOK

well beaten by good balls that shaved the stumps in the first moments of their durance at the wicket. Even after these cricketers had worked hard to blunt the English bowling, it came along again with new vigour. At ten minutes to four Australia had seven men out for 271—no great achievement on a perfect ground. Armstrong himself was urged from his customary ease to get Australia quite on the safe way. Not once did the English bowlers admit rebuff; they had no thunderbolts, or few, to serve out, but they fought with big hearts, though the day's usage must have told them again and again that it was Australia's fortunate season, that good luck, as her way is, waited on superiority. In the reproof of chance, though, lies the true proof of men: on Saturday the scorching ordeal found an English team braver than the Nottingham and Lord's teams—one lacking little of determination and philosophy, whatever it may have lacked of the habit of victory.

The fall of Australia's wickets tells the tale of the changefulness of England's hopes:—

1	2	3	4	5	6	7	8	9	10
22	45	146	255	256	271	271	333	388	407

Bardsley and Andrews fell to beautiful slip catches by Woolley in the first hour, sent from Douglas's nineteenth and forty-first balls. Douglas, who opened the English bowling with J. C. White, had 49 runs hit from his first ten overs, but if only because he got rid of Bardsley, by a ball that swung away beautifully from the bat, he did his side some service. With Macartney and Pellew in, both "ware and waking," sniffing danger for Australia in the air, Douglas put in all of his strength and pugnacity to keep the foe under, now that it was for the nonce laid fairly low. The sixth ball he sent to Macartney pitched outside the wicket, and broke back, just to miss the off bail by an inch. The third ball he sent to Pellew came from the turf at a fine pace, broke through the batsman's defence irresistibly—and also grazed the wicket but did not break it. And Pellew and Macartney then added 101 runs for the third Australian wicket! Pellew drove strongly in front of the wicket, but many a hit did he make in desperation, trusting to the favourable gods. Taylor was Macartney's next helpmate, and between them they added 109 for the fourth Australian wicket. Taylor was less than a dozen when a lovely break-back from Douglas consternated him, beat his bat, hit him on the right thigh, and missed the wicket by a fraction. With his score 22 Taylor gave a " return " chance to White, who dropped the ball. In the same over White missed a hard chance sent by Macartney, who now was 79. All of these straws that showed the way of the wind, how it blew in Australia's way.

Taylor was caught neatly by Douglas with the Australian total 255. Then Parkin ran amuck for a period. In three overs he clean bowled Gregory and Hendry, uprooting wickets, and also got the conquering Macartney "l.b.w." Parkin, in this happy spell, bowled very fast, found a length just short of a convenient forward stroke, and caused the ball to

A CRICKETER'S BOOK

keep low surprisingly. He promised us an overthrow in quick time of the Australian rearguard, but we reckoned without our Armstrong, who really is a great batsman still—when circumstances prick him on. Armstrong ambled to the wicket on Saturday just after half-past three, gave a large magnanimous smile at the destroying Parkin, and then proceeded to hit Parkin heftily to the on boundary time after time, scalding himself by the violent motion of his work, but plainly to his enjoyment. Armstrong drives to the on side with perhaps more power than any other man in the game to-day. He accomplishes the might of it from two legs stupendously astride the crease (the old Shakespearian echo comes up inevitably as one beholds him), his bat swinging with the majesty of some elemental movement, some turning-about of nature. Armstrong, though, has science in his furious work: he is no iconoclast. There is true gospel in his batsmanship: he serves you out the orthodox in hard apostolic knocks. On Saturday he hit a six and ten fours, batted 90 minutes for his 77, scored 48 out of 55 after the tea interval. Carter, always a thorn in England's side, helped Armstrong to add 62 for the eighth wicket, and Macdonald helped him to add 55 for the ninth. Even Mailey, in last of all, gave a hint of batsmanship by a gorgeous drive to the leg boundary.

Yet all these fine happenings in the Australian rearguard came through the skill of Macartney, who for three hours and ten minutes played beautiful cricket, and wooed his good luck like a happy cavalier. Macartney was the fount that made the small brooks to flow for Australia. He came in to bat at a critical point, and, all in all, played so sweet and clever a game that he deserved his occasional gifts from the gods. It was not Macartney quite in his " cheekiest " vein. He did not behave in the cock-a-hoop way that led to his undoing at Lord's the other week. To bat three hours and score only a hundred or so is sedate going for Macartney. Perhaps Armstrong had informed him on Saturday morning that a Test match, after all, *is* a Test match, with proprieties in it to be observed.

Yet though Macartney so curbed the inveterate imp at the bottom of him that he did not once try to cut a ball from the middle stump, this same imp would now and again break out, however solemn the hour, in some impudent trafficking at an off-ball—some coxcombry, with a cross bat, to the on side. In such moments—when the irrepressible spirit of Macartney peeped out—one thought of Till Eulenspiegel under the very eye of the judge. But perhaps there is something too lightsome, too airy and graceful in Macartney's impishness, to suit the comparison with the Teuton Till. Shall we call him the Figaro of batsmen—that is Mozart's Figaro? His boundary strokes on Saturday were six cuts through the slips, one straight drive rather to the on-side, three drives through the covers, two square-leg hits, and a lucky snick behind the wicket. His famous stroke through the slips one must for convenience's sake call a late cut, but the term in its customary significance does not fit. This stroke is not made at the last minute, as the ball passes the wicket, in the way of an afterthought. It is not a back stroke at all, but essentially forward in spirit and technique. The footwork of the hit suggests a drive in front of point, only Macartney waits a little later, and, using his bat in a horizontal plane, quite definitely drives the ball (hitting it seemingly not on top but on the side) to the left of point, wide of the wicket, but none the less behind it. The stroke is not a slash at the ball's pitch, but deliberate, and perfectly safe. It is brilliant and powerful, and if Macartney were to make it once only in a long innings it would " sign " the innings as unmistakably as Whistler's butterfly signs a painting.

The English bowlers did their best. Nothing that was in them did not come out. Douglas, of course, captained the side after Tennyson's mishap (men propose but the gods dispose!), and on the whole handled his attack satisfactorily. Parkin did good work at intervals, with atrocious luck. Douglas, too, deserved better results. Jupp, for a while after lunch, had pace from the pitch, and an occasional off-break. White, the new International bowler, was pretty to watch. His work had a touch of art in it despite (or because of, as Oscar Wilde would have urged) its uselessness as an attacking force. The curve of his flight was graceful, and the motion of his action had rhythm. He bowls left arm, slow to slow medium, skilfully disguises his flight and pitch, swings in to the wicket at times and at others defi-

LEEDS

nitely breaks in by a leg break spin not often employed by left-arm bowlers. On Saturday his pace from the wicket was not fast enough; the batsmen could safely play a defensive half-cock at the last moment, whenever the flight had set them guessing beforehand. On hard wickets one can well imagine White troubling inexperienced batsmen, but he will need more " nip " from the turf than on Saturday to worry the Australians on hard grounds.

England's fielding was variable. Hallows, acting as substitute for Tennyson, was as good as anybody. Douglas did useful work on the leg side, and Woolley in the slips was lithe and dependable. Ducat and Jupp misfielded occasionally. Brown behind the wicket rarely made a mistake, though it seemed that so superb a fieldsman as he might have caught Macartney at 62. Brown allowed no byes until over 200 runs were scored, and what balls did pass him after that were violently erratic. Woolley and Hearne were bowled by sheer pace in a dubious light.

A CRICKETER'S BOOK

SECOND DAY, JULY 4th, 1921.

(Scores at Close of Play.)

AUSTRALIANS.

First Innings.		Second Innings.	
W. Bardsley, c Woolley, b Douglas	6	b Jupp	25
T. J. Andrews, c Woolley, b Douglas	19	not out	78
C. G. Macartney, lbw, b Parkin	115	c and b Woolley	80
C. E. Pellew, c Hearne. b Woolley	52		
J. M. Taylor, c Douglas, b Jupp	50		
J. M. Gregory, b Parkin	1		
H. L. Hendry, b Parkin	0		
W. W. Armstrong, c Brown, b Douglas	77		
H. Carter, b Jupp	34	not out	3
E. A. Macdonald, not out	21		
A. A. Mailey, c and b Parkin	6		
Extras	26	Extras	7
Total	407	Total (for 2 wkts.)	143

ENGLAND—First Innings.

Woolley, b Gregory	0
Hardinge, lbw, b Armstrong	25
Hearne, b Macdonald	7
Ducat, c Gregory, b Macdonald	3
J. W. H. T. Douglas, b Armstrong	75
V. W. C. Jupp, c Carter, b Gregory	14
Brown, c Armstrong, b Mailey	57
J. C. White, b Macdonald	1
L. H. Tennyson, c Gregory, b Macdonald	63
Parkin, not out	5
Hobbs, absent	0
Extras	9
Total	259

This morning there was none of the sunshine that warmed the Australians' holiday on Saturday. The sky was grey and a chill wind blew. And it blew

LEEDS

more and more of shabby fortune for England. The vast crowd was afflicted at the outset by the tidings that Hobbs would not use his bat for us to-day, for his indisposition of the week-end had made an unhappy development, so much so that an operation upon him was urgent. The surgeons did their work on the greatest batsman of them all at mid-day, just as the battle went its hardest against his side. But this was but a part of the ill-luck the wind went on sending in for England—as east a wind as ever the gentleman in Dickens discovered. In the first quarter of an hour of cricket, Ducat and Hardinge, both playing well, were out by the sheerest interferences from the imps of mischief. Ducat, with his side's total 30, sought to place a fast ball from Macdonald through the slips. The stroke was in good style, but alack, the ball struck a flaw in the willow which, splintering, robbed the hit of all power, changing it to the tamest slip catch. Seventeen runs later than this, Hardinge was given out leg before wicket to a slow dropping ball from Armstrong. Hardinge's impression yet is that he played the ball hard, and he can produce excellent witnesses to the fact. Was ever a team struggling hard for Test match honours, matched against a strong, ruthless foe, so churlishly whipped as this by the gods?

Just as the clocks struck noon it seemed all too certain that again we were to witness a complete overthrow of England. Five wickets were down for 67, and not only was Hobbs out of action but, as everybody believed then, Tennyson too. Then as the very air hummed with things bodeful for England, the tide turned. It turned even as softly and as secretly as the sea's tide—it was a change deeply hidden, and none of us quite saw the current moving England's way till, in the afternoon, it gathered in motion and Tennyson himself rode on the waters gloriously.

The Australian onrush was stopped by Brown and Douglas. These two cricketers joined in defence at ten minutes to twelve, with the England score 67 for five wickets, and they batted most doggedly till half-past two, taking the total to 165, thus establishing the biggest partnership made in an English Test match innings this summer, so far. Armstrong used all of his resources to rid himself of these obstructing men, but in vain. Neither Brown nor Douglas gave a hint that they intended to leave the wicket. When Brown at last got out it was through his own folly; he hit incautiously at a long hop. Still, as one has said, it was but slowly that the course of England's fortune changed. At a quarter to three, when White was bowled neck and crop, England had two wickets only in keeping—one of them a man with a crippled hand; and a formidable matter of 92 had to be got over to save the follow-on and so cultivate a chance of forcing a draw on Armstrong. And the heavy task was done, a haven reached in the turmoil for awhile. Tennyson's last-minute rally to-day might have moved his poetic ancestor to lofty verse, though only the majestic cadences of his " Ulysses " would do suitable honour. For Tennyson, with his left hand all bandages and coming to the wicket late in the innings, just gave a cavalier smile at the enclosing gloom, and, to the joy, aye, and the bewilderment of the multitude, straightway attacked the Australian fast bowlers, and his bat, all curves and thrusts, flashed the ball to the remote parts of the field.

English cricketers will by no means encourage a churl to suggest they are thankful for small mercies if they make a great epic out of this little innings by Tennyson. Not one of the conquering Australians indeed is there that would not be proud to tell and re-tell the fame of it all. Tennyson in a ruinous hour for his side, to the accompaniment of stabs of pain from the wounded hand, yet played the happy wayfarer, and again he blazoned the news to the land that a big heart will take one a long way against these Australians. Tennyson came in to bat when Douglas was 51 and the total score 166. He drove to the off and glided through the slips to such tune that he made 62 while Douglas made 24. He put Gregory and Macdonald to flight by hitting eight fours from their fast bowling. He had a fortunate escape behind the wicket now and then, and gave a chance to the bowler at ten, but well did he deserve to prosper. Tennyson, in all, batted some eighty minutes and scored 63 out of 106. This is the sequence of his strokes :—2, 2, 1, 1, 4, 4, 4, 4, 4, 2, 3, 1, 4, 4, 1, 1, 1, 4, 2, 4, 1, 1, 1, 4, 2, 1.

With all its gusto there was yet plenty of the marks of culture in Tennyson's batsmanship. He showed us all that a man can drive one-handed even if he will get quickly into the right position for driving. His footwork had quickness always, and the classical left leg motion was in every hit to the off side, the forward foot pointing in the way of the ball's direction. He rose high on his toes to the fast bowlers' bumpers and played them down with a left elbow beautifully up. Tennyson returned to the pavilion, at the end of his fine adventure, to the wildest cheering one has heard on a cricket field for long days. There was, indeed, plenty of Yorkshire roars as the England innings burned out in glory. When Parkin came in, last man of all, four runs were needed still to save the follow-on, and as he smote a ball from Armstrong to the on-boundary some 26,000 folk made tremendous noises. But it is hardly likely Armstrong would have sent England in again—his bowlers were well spent at the finish.

The sturdy batsmanship of Brown and Douglas was for a period put out of mind by the fine rapture of Tennyson. But the quality of it must have left its impression firmly on the mind of everybody that watched the cricket. The vigilance of Douglas was unwearying, his spirit indomitable throughout. He was the watch-dog Kurneval, patient for a sign of good fortune coming, while his master saw one in a fine passionate fever. He batted for four hours, was patient and skilful while 222 runs were scored. He hit six boundaries. His bat was in an immaculate perpendicular whenever a straight ball came in. Brown was, of course, using his bat for the first time in a Test match. The game's situation, when he came to the wicket, might well have unnerved him. But he is a big, raw-boned man, and seemingly very sure of himself. He arrived at the crease and surveyed the Australians with a hang-dog sort of air, as who should say, " I've heard all about these Test matches, but I'm going to have a look at 'em for myself." Plainly he was sceptical of the reputation of Australian bowling. True he sampled it warily at the outset, but quite composedly. And, having satisfied himself, he proceeded to force it to the front of the wicket. Brown is a natural cricketer, who plainly has been nicely coached. He has a good reach and depends largely on a forward technique both in attack and defence. To-day he was on view for one hour and forty minutes, and made his 50 out of 84.

The Australian bowling was deadly enough in the first two hours of the day. Then, both Macdonald and Gregory had great pace and both broke back viciously at times. But after lunch, when Douglas and Tennyson were batting, it had a definitely crumpled aspect. Gregory and Macdonald lost their lengths; in 17 overs 71 runs were hit from these bowlers, among them eleven boundary hits. The crowd sighed, " Oh, for Hobbs now."

Australia, leading by 148, pressed home the advantage by saucy batsmanship at the afternoon's fall. Still, granted a fair wicket to-morrow, England might find it within her power to force a draw. England five for 67 and 259 for nine—what a great-hearted

A CRICKETER'S BOOK

rally here, and in circumstances heavy enough to break the bravest spirit! The lessons of to-day's cricket will not be lost; we are slowly finding these Australians out. Let Tennyson only go on along his dauntless way. And for his watchword there are lines in his grandfather's volumes:—

> Tho' much is taken, much abides; and tho'
> We are not now that strength which in old days
> Moved earth and heaven; that which we are, we are;
> One equal temper of heroic hearts.

THIRD AND LAST DAY, JULY 5th, 1921.

(Final Scores.)

AUSTRALIANS.

First Innings.		Second Innings.	
W. Bardsley, c Woolley, b Douglas	6	b Jupp	25
T. J. Andrews, c Woolley, b Douglas	19	b Jupp	92
C. G. Macartney, lbw, b Parkin	115	c and b Woolley	30
C. E. Pellew, c Hearne, b Woolley	52	c Ducat, b White	16
J. M. Taylor, c Douglas, b Jupp	50	c Tennyson, b White	4
J. M. Gregory, b Parkin	1	c Jupp, b White	3
H. L. Hendry, b Parkin	0	not out	11
W. W. Armstrong, c Brown, b Douglas	77	not out	28
H. Carter, b Jupp	34	lbw, b Parkin	47
E. A. Macdonald, not out	21		
A. A. Mailey, c and b Parkin	6		
Extras	26	Extras	17
Total	407	Total (for 7 wkts.)	273
		(Innings declared closed.)	

LEEDS

ENGLAND.

First Innings.		Second Innings.	
Woolley, b Gregory	0	b Mailey	87
Hardinge, lbw, b Armstrong	25	c Gregory, b Macdonald	5
Hearne, b Macdonald	7	c Taylor, b Macdonald	27
Ducat, c Gregory, b Macdonald	8	st Carter, b Mailey	2
J. W. H. T. Douglas, b Armstrong	75	b Gregory	8
V. W. C. Jupp, c Carter, b Gregory	14	c Carter, b Armstrong	28
Brown, c Armstrong, b Mailey	57	lbw, b Gregory	46
J. C. White, b Macdonald	1	not out	6
L. H. Tennyson, c Gregory, b Macdonald	63	b Armstrong	36
Parkin, not out	5	b Mailey	4
Hobbs, absent	0	absent	0
Extras	9	Extras	3
Total	259	Total	202

ENGLAND BOWLING—First Innings.

	O.	M.	R.	W.		O.	M.	R.	W.
Douglas	20	3	80	3	Hearne	5	0	21	0
White	25	4	70	0	Jupp	18	2	70	2
Parkin	20.1	0	106	4	Woolley	5	0	34	1

Second Innings.

	O.	M.	R.	W.		O.	M.	R.	W.
Douglas	11	0	38	0	Jupp	13	2	45	2
White	11	3	37	3	Woolley	18	4	45	1
Parkin	20	0	91	1					

AUSTRALIAN BOWLING—First Innings.

	O.	M.	R.	W.		O.	M.	R.	W.
Gregory	21	6	47	2	Mailey	17	4	38	1
Macdonald	26.1	0	105	4	Hendry	10	4	16	0
Armstrong	19	4	44	2					

Second Innings.

	O.	M.	R.	W.		O.	M.	R.	W.
Gregory	14	1	55	2	Mailey	20.2	3	71	3
Macdonald	15	2	67	2	Armstrong	3	0	6	2

A CRICKETER'S BOOK

The ashes remain with Armstrong. England lost this game at five o'clock to-day by 219 runs, and moreover lost it rather weakly. Armstrong closed the Australian second innings at one o'clock, and thirteen minutes later England went in to bat again, 421 behind, with nearly five hours left for cricket. The English innings had a poor prelude, for Hardinge got himself out through an indiscreet stroke in the slips with the score 15 only. Brown and Hearne then raised hopes by taking the total to 57 in little more than half an hour. The cricket of these men was so easeful that a newcomer to the scene might have imagined that England was the conquering side. But just as Hearne seemed thoroughly settled down, and we were all looking at his comfortable stance at the wicket and praising his pretty and composed batsmanship, he got out by some sudden absence of mind—playing a ball from Macdonald most gently to mid-on's hands. With Woolley and Brown in companionship, though, we could again hope on, for there was some confidence in the cricket of both of them.

Gregory and Macdonald were put out of action. Macdonald, in ten overs after lunch, had 48 runs hit from his bowling, and Gregory was hit for 11 in three overs. Armstrong did not like the way of events just now, and asked Mailey to bowl. Not often this summer has Armstrong turned first of all to Mailey when his fast bowlers have failed him. And yesterday his choice of Mailey as first change bowler, in preference to Hendry or himself, was an inspiration. Everything " comes off " for Armstrong.

LEEDS

Mailey, who has not been a consistently good bowler this summer, contrived on this critical occasion to jump at Armstrong's cue like the Catastrophe in the old comedies. He discovered a length and gave the ball a rare spin and pace from the pitch. It was Gregory, though, that upset the vital Woolley-Brown partnership, for he claimed Brown leg before wicket. Then Mailey set about puzzling the batsmen, and with England's score 124 he confounded Woolley into a poor stroke. It may be said that into Woolley's downfall some element entered of the illfortune that has dogged England consistently throughout this game. He played the ball on to his body, and it rolled from it on to the wicket. Still, the stroke he used hardly deserved a better fate. Woolley was fourth out at 124, and the time was 8.40.

A chance for England to save the game remained—granted that Ducat could reproduce his county form. But this he failed most lamentably to do. To Mailey he behaved like a man sorely perplexed, and soon jumped out desperately to a perfectly-pitched spinning ball, missed it, and departed stumped. The value of Mailey's bowling to Australia is not to be reckoned entirely by the number of wickets that came his way. His amazing spin unsettled the minds of the batsmen even when they managed to play him. Jupp and Tennyson fought a plucky rearguard action and at the tea interval both of them were undefeated, the score reading England 190 for six. But the Australians can invariably discover in a rest for sustenance rare recuperative power. Twenty balls after tea were ample to bring in England's downfall. The last three wickets fell for a paltry dozen runs, and so the game went out like a damp squib.

Much may be made of the fact that to the end England was harried by the whips of fortune. This morning Douglas learned that his wife, like Hobbs, was a victim to appendicitis and stood urgently in need of an operation. When Douglas came in to bat he was plainly over-weighted by anxiety. Moreover, Brown strained his leg during the Australian second innings and had to employ Hallows as a runner when he batted. Let these unhappy mishaps go to the long roll of England's buffetings from the fates. Yet the truth comes out—that the very cricketers most afflicted by luck were those to play the bravest cricket. Tennyson and Brown with painful limbs could make runs, while able-bodied men like Ducat and Hardinge couldn't. It is all the more unpalatable to tell the tale of England's defeat to-day, for the reason that Gregory and Macdonald both were definitely below themselves. In the match Australia's fast bowlers were hit for some 270 runs and they managed to get but ten men out between them. Even Mailey this afternoon, well as he bowled, achieved nothing that is not common to the googly bowler's arts. The English cricketers were sadly at fault in the methods they used against him. Forward play is not the specific for the ball that spins " the other way." The lunge at a ball's pitch is permissible only when you are sure that the ball on pitching will follow along the line of flight.

LEEDS

To a bowler who is concealing his spin's direction the safe way is back play—unless you have the quick feet of Trumper and Hobbs. To-day the bulk of England's batsmen tackled Mailey with the right foot immovable on the earth, thrusting out with the left in sheer speculation. The wonder is that Mailey did not get a fine harvest of wickets.

England's collapse, following the brave batsmanship of Tennyson, Brown, and Douglas yesterday, left the crowd dumb and disconsolate. Again Brown and Tennyson played plucky cricket. Brown had not only pluck but uncommon skill. His strained leg gave him a twinge at every vigorous hit, but he stuck to his game resolutely. When he was batting the Australian bowling had quite a commonplace look.

The Australian innings earlier in the day was none too good, and thereby hangs a significant moral. At the morning's outset the turf, under the influence of dew, allowed the bowlers to spin the ball, and so incompetently did Andrews and others shape against Woolley that one was forced to the view that in a wet —that is a typical—English summer the Australians might very well get into grave trouble. Andrews just missed his century, but though his cricket on the fast wicket of Monday afternoon had excellent points, his lack of ability against the turning ball to-day quite prevents one from putting him amongst fully equipped batsmen. With Woolley's best bowling he often made an elementary mistake. Woolley now and again sent him a ball of difficult length for a forward stroke, which after pitching on the off stump broke abruptly away from the bat. And Andrews invariably sought to play it by a speculative push stroke, which found the ball just at the dangerous point of the break—that is, at the beginning. A batsman properly acquainted with a bowler's wicket would have held back till the ball pitched and the spin had finished its work, and would have placed it through the slips—the stroke taking much the course that the ball took after turning. Andrews this morning was by no means on a wicket definitely sticky—the dew's influence was not heavy and it soon passed away. Yet Woolley had him on pins all the time he was batting, and with some luck would have bowled him at least thrice. Carter, too, was unskilful and fortunate. He is of the company of cricketers who get runs though they cannot bat. Parkin bowled cleverly for a while at the beginning of the day, but his quick off-break needed a better length.

Once this morning it seemed likely the Australians would be all out for a moderate score. The fourth wicket fell at 223, and then three others went for only seven runs. White for a while had a prosperous season, three wickets falling to him for a single run. But the Australians now were hitting at nearly everything, and Armstrong found little difficulty by means of a judicious game to stop the rot and to drive the bowling powerfully in front of the wicket. Hendry, by grace of Providence, managed to keep his captain company till the declaration. White's bowling to-day is likely to be over-valued. He managed his slow in-swinger well enough, but there is neither the craft nor the spin from the wicket in his work necessary to worry first-class cricketers. Brown, again, was a dexterous stumper.

CHAPTER IV

MANCHESTER

FIRST DAY, JULY 25th, 1921.
(Scores at Close of Play.)

ENGLAND—First Innings.

Brown, c Gregory, b Armstrong	31
Russell, b Gregory	101
Woolley, c Pellew, b Armstrong	41
Mead, c Andrews, b Hendry	47
Tyldesley (E.), not out	78
P. G. H. Fender, not out	44
Extras	20
Total (for four wickets)	362

After a day which went far to clear the character of our batsmanship this summer in Test matches, English cricket suffered a nasty shock to its pride at the afternoon's very fall. And so it happened that instead of one finding oneself for the nonce able to go home from a Test match rejoicing to the full that England yet has her strong men, the pleasure was just slightly disturbed by the thought that it had needed the Australian captain to bring us back to a proper intimacy with our own laws of cricket.

For at ten minutes to six Tennyson sought to declare his innings closed with the English total 341 for four wickets. He came on the field and waved Tyldesley and Fender back to the pavilion. One noted that Armstrong protested against this signal.

MANCHESTER

He left the field, though, and the matter was argued out. After some twenty minutes' stoppage of the game Armstrong led his men to the field again and the English innings had to go on. A section of the crowd behaved rather disgracefully. Armstrong was barracked as he attempted to continue the Australian bowling. Whereupon he sat down heavily on the grass—as massive and concrete as Mr Wopsle himself. Tennyson and Street were compelled to put the crowd to some quietude by an explanation.

Armstrong acted quite in accordance with the laws of English cricket. Law 55 declares that when there is no play on the first day of a three-day match Law 54 shall apply as if the match were a two-day match. Law 54 states that in a two-day match the captain of the batting side has power to declare his innings at a close at any time, "but such declaration may not be made on the first day later than one hour and forty minutes before the time agreed upon for drawstumps." It is plain, then, according to the laws of the game as conceived by English cricket authorities, that Tennyson was acting illegally in attempting to close his innings as late in the afternoon as ten minutes to 6, there having been no cricket on Saturday. He had no legal right to delay his closure after ten minutes to five. The unruly part of the crowd asked Armstrong in loud voices to "play the game." As a fact, he *was* playing the game by insisting on an observance by English cricketers of English cricket laws. Armstrong found himself placed in a difficult position, but it is hard to see that any course other than the one he adopted was open to him.*

The day's play had fine moments for English cricketers. At last we have seen the Australian bowlers steadfastly opposed, at last we have seen the Australian fieldsmen very definitely " on the run "— and a little moist with the sweat of hard labour. The cricket exposed the weak point in the Australian team. They are obviously not a side likely to pass invincibly through a wet summer. They plainly do not possess bowling good enough for slow easy-paced wickets. On this occasion Macdonald was compelled to emulate medium-paced bowling. Gregory, too, bowled well below his customary pace—and he has not Macdonald's command over spin and flight. Armstrong and Hendry worked hard, but Armstrong was forced by the batsmen to exploit defensive tactics. He plainly gave up as a bad job the problem of getting men out and persisted in length bowling well away from the wicket—content merely to keep runs down. Hendry is not better than a county bowler of every-day class, and Macartney— the one left-handed bowler on view yesterday—has lost his old-time break and flight.

The English batsmen jumped at the opportunity joyfully. At the outset the runs did not come furiously, but Brown and Russell had a knowing air about them as who should say " There's no devil in the wicket and no Trumble about with the devil in his

* In the confusion Armstrong was permitted to bowl two overs in succession—one before the interruption and one after. But few people in the crowd " tumbled " to this lapse—at the moment.

MANCHESTER

own fingers!" Yet, but for the grace of Providence, Russell might have gone the way of most of England's first-wicket batsmen in Test cricket this summer, with his score an insignificant six. For then he snicked a rising ball from Gregory to Armstrong, whose left hand could not grip the flying ball. Brown and Russell scored 65 for England's first wicket—the happiest prelude to an English innings this summer. Brown, as at Leeds, was all confidence. He is a cricketer that comes close to nature —one as hard as a tree and as much the work of the elements. His downfall yesterday came through sheer exuberance. He smote a ball from Armstrong to the leg boundary, and sought to do it all over again from the next ball, but hit the ball straight to Gregory. There was sage talk in the crowd about Armstrong's gins and snares; in this instance, it is possible Armstrong owed as much for his overthrow of Brown to the lucky stars as to his "old soldier" ways.

The sequence of the fall of England's wickets yesterday show how hard the Australians had to work to make headway:—

1	2	3	4
65	145	217	260

At lunch England's score was 143 for one wicket. It was expected that with so solid a foundation to the innings as this achieved, the English batsmen would proceed immediately after lunch to force the advantage home, attack the Australian bowling vigorously, and so give a chance to Tennyson of an early declaration. That Tennyson was compelled to wait until the illegal hour of ten minutes to six before he could safely put an end to his innings was in measure the fault of Mead and Russell after the interval. Both men played an unenterprising game. Mead needed one hour and a half for the making of 30; Russell was somnolent for 85 minutes, and scored 25 only. Woolley, who threw his wicket away playing the right game for England, promised a beautiful innings. He came to the wicket at a quarter-past twelve, and made four most elegant fast-footed drives. Alas, when he went in to lunch he might well have said, like the lady in Ford's play: " There's but a dining time 'twixt me and my confusion." In Armstrong's second over after lunch he drove a ball to Pellew into deep field, and Pellew did not need to move an inch to catch it.

Mead observed the unities of his art conscientiously. He is Clement Hill without the punch. Russell scored a century, and had he forced the game in the later stages of his innings one would be compelled to praise his work without stint. He is definitely a modern batsman in his preference of on-side over off-side play. Yesterday his score was 75 before he made a real hit in the direction of cover point. There is too much of fore-arm action in his strokes for grace; his body does not swing rhythmically into a hit. His fine points are watchfulness and an erect poise as he plays the ball. He batted four hours yesterday for 101, made out of a total of 216. Armstrong missed him for the second time with his score 86.

Russell did his side service in blunting what of edge there was on the Australian bowling at the day's beginning. He was out at five minutes to four, and then Ernest Tyldesley's innings came—and for the while he put Russell and his utility out of mind. Tyldesley did not breed confidence straightway; for half an hour his strokes had no resolution; that half-cock stroke of his, made, it would seem, with a measure of philosophic doubt sweeping over him, was painfully notable. Then, with Fender in, playing "under orders to hit," the spirit of J. T. Tyldesley entered into his brother. After the tea interval Ernest Tyldesley burned the gem-like flame: the grey day was shot with a white dazzling light. His cricket had in it a forcefulness and audacity. It was *picaresque*; Tyldesley passed with true arrogance along the gay road, the happy philanderer. We had witnessed Russell and Mead go before him through the straight gate, making virtuous movement onwards, "little by little," and this decline of Tyldesley's from cold rectitude was welcome. Tyldesley snapped fingers at the proprieties. He hooked—he pulled; he cut fast balls that were still rising as they passed the wickets; he jumped to length balls, made half-volleys of them, and drove them wantonly right and left. In 30 minutes after the tea interval Tyldesley scored 48 out of 65—and the swashbuckling Fender at the other end, at that. His hits from tea time till the "declaration" mis-

A CRICKETER'S BOOK

adventure were these—2, 1, 2, 2, 1, 1, 4, 1, 4, 1, 1, 4, 1, 1, 4, 2, 2, 4, 6, 1, 4, 4, 1. The crescendo took the crowd to the heights. He smote a ball from Hendry to the top of the awning in the ladies' pavilion. He hit boundaries from Gregory and Macdonald, cuts, off-drives, and pulls. He has never played a finer game, even at Old Trafford; yesterday he was, indeed, J. T. Tyldesley's own brother.

The Australian fielding was good, but not always touching their own Test match standard. Pellew and Taylor in the deep field were brilliant, and the vigilance of the grey little man Carter never wavered.

SECOND DAY, JULY 26th, 1921.

(Final Scores.)

ENGLAND—First Innings.

Brown, c Gregory, b Armstrong	31
Russell, b Gregory	101
Woolley, c Pellew, b Armstrong	41
Mead, c Andrews, b Hendry	47
Tyldesley (E.), not out	78
P. G. H. Fender, not out	44
Extras	20
Total (for four wickets)	362

(Innings declared.)

L. H. Tennyson, J. W. H. T. Douglas, Hallows, Parkin, and Parker did not bat.

Second Innings.

Hallows, not out	16
Parkin, c Collins, b Andrews	23
Parker, not out	3
Extras	2
Total (for one wicket)	44

MANCHESTER

AUSTRALIA—First Innings.

H. L. Collins, lbw, b Parkin	40
W. Bardsley, b Parkin	3
C. G. Macartney, b Parker	13
T. J. E. Andrews, c Tennyson. b Fender	6
J. M. Taylor, b Fender	4
C. E. Pellew, c Tyldesley, b Parker	17
W. W. Armstrong, b Douglas	17
J. M. Gregory, b Parkin	29
H. Carter, b Parkin	0
H. L. Hendry, c Russell, b Parkin	4
E. A. Macdonald, not out	8
Extras	34
Total	175

AUSTRALIAN BOWLING—First Innings.

	O.	M.	R.	W.		O.	M.	R.	W.
Gregory	23	5	79	1	Armstrong	33	13	57	2
Macdonald	31	1	112	0	Hendry	25	5	74	1
Macartney	8	2	20	0					

Second Innings.

	O.	M.	R.	W.		O.	M.	R.	W.
Hendry	4	1	12	0	Pellew	3	0	6	0
Andrews	5	0	23	1	Taylor	1	0	1	0

ENGLAND BOWLING—First Innings.

	O.	M.	R.	W.		O.	M.	R.	W.
Parkin	29.4	12	38	5	Fender	15	6	30	2
Woolley	39	22	38	0	Douglas	5	2	3	1
Parker	28	16	32	2					

There was the scourge intolerable and the torturing hour at Old Trafford on this closing day of the fourth Test match. There were, in fact, five torturing hours, in which Collins defended his wicket and made no more runs than 40. Australia saved the game, thanks mainly to the amazing vigilance of this cricketer, who was, indeed, patience on a monument —without a smile of any sort. It was half-past five

A CRICKETER'S BOOK

before England rid themselves of the last Australian wicket, and the Australian innings amounted to 175, scored at the rate (one will not say pace) of little more than 30 an hour.

The big crowd gave itself over frankly to affliction. For a while irony was directed in ample quantities at Collins. A voice from the heart of the multitude warned him that if he did not hurry up he would " miss the boat home." But Collins went his patient way; the irony was lost on him. He proceeded by rapt and not very æsthetic rote (if **Mr** Hardy will excuse a variation on a fine phrase) to place the crowd in a condition of nice catalepsy. The scoffers gave up the unequal contest and went to sleep. Collins, of course, played a useful game for his side. An amount of responsibility was put on him at the outset of Australia's innings, for Bardsley and Macartney were out at mid-day. These cricketers and himself and Armstrong are the only batsmen of reliability on his side familiar with an English drying wicket. Had he failed straightway who knows how dangerously Australia might have been pressed? Events at the end of the Australian innings went some way to justify Collins's yawn-compelling game; when he departed at five o'clock the Australian innings collapsed.

Yet it did seem that the Australians magnified their troubles. The wicket was never difficult, and, frankly, the English bowling fell disappointingly below Test match standards. No hot sun shone to make the moist turf " bite," though the ball could

MANCHESTER

be made to spin by a skilful bowler, if not to spin viciously. Parkin, unfortunately, was the only English bowler who made good use of what existed in the wicket in the way of venom. The Australians, then, might well have cultivated a more adventuresome game than they did, without jeopardy to their chances of saving the match. At 3.30 they had surely passed out of the danger zone, with a first innings score of 120 for five on the board. Only some three hours remained for cricket now, and Armstrong and his men had 15 wickets in keeping. Yet did the Australians continue to look upon Woolley's penny-plain slow bowling suspiciously. The English bowlers must have felt flattered at the respect paid to them; on Monday England's batsmen on a wicket of much the same order had scored heavily. Still, the timid aspect of Australia yesterday was good to behold, after Lord's, Trent Bridge, and Leeds. Moreover the wary methods of the Australians gave a sense to the day's play that it was vital, though it would be hard to prove that England ever stood a fair chance on the wicket of upsetting twenty good batsmen in less than seven hours.

The best bowling of the day was by Parkin. He set about Bardsley at the morning's beginning with the air of a match-winner. His length was good and his off-break accurately directed. A break-back that whipped from the pitch at a rare pace clean bowled Bardsley in his third over. Parkin's bowling always had rare spin in it; now and then perhaps it was just a shade too much on the short side to get the bats-

A CRICKETER'S BOOK

men " guessing." Still, he was so plainly the most skilful of England's bowlers that it is a pity Tennyson did not put as much confidence in him as he did in Woolley, who in the innings was asked to bowl ten overs more than Parkin. Woolley had little of Rhodes's cunning. He extracted no amount of spin from the pitch and little of generalship went into his management of length and flight. Parker was the better left-handed man of the two. His length was always good, and he bowled the ball that " goes with the arm " at a low and deceptive flight. Still, he did not get the amount of spin in his bowling that one has a right to expect from a medium-paced Test match bowler on a drying wicket.

The quality of Fender's bowling was variable. An excellent break-back upset Taylor's wicket. Taken in the lump, he had little of spin or of troublesome length. Douglas was not put on to bowl till Australia's score was 120 and the time nearly half-past three. He bore up well under the unfamiliar experience, and when at last Tennyson asked him to bowl he broke through Armstrong's guard in his third over. Armstrong batted an hour for 17, and Pellew toiled for an hour and twenty minutes for 17. It was Pellew who, with Collins, blunted the edge of England's bowling before lunch. He went to the wicket at half-past twelve, with the Australian score 48 for four wickets, and he stayed there till twenty minutes after the lunch interval. There was merit in his careful cricket, for Pellew is at heart an adventurer in the game—a Cavalier, not a Roundhead.

MANCHESTER

The English fielding was competent, though Brown did not keep wicket as skilfully as at Leeds. When Australia's innings collapsed after the tea interval—Parkin finished it off in seven overs, taking four wickets for ten runs—it was expected that Australia would bat again. But Tennyson spared the crowd from suffering another dose of Collins. England had little to gain by attacking the Australian batsmen a second time, since less than three-quarters of an hour now remained for cricket. Tennyson mercifully provided an anodyne for the pains inflicted on the crowd during the Australian innings by sending Parkin with Hallows " to bat time out." And so we have lived to see Parkin go in first for England !

CHAPTER V

KENNINGTON OVAL

FIRST DAY, AUGUST 13th, 1921.
(Score at Close of Play.)

ENGLAND—First Innings.

Brown, b Mailey	82
Russell, c Oldfield, b Macdonald	13
Tyldesley, c Macartney, b Gregory	39
Woolley, run out	28
Mead, not out	19
Sandham, not out	1
Extras	2
Total (for four wickets)	129

The wonderful London summer rather collapsed to-day, and there was only some two hours and three-quarter's play at the Oval in the prelude of the last Test match. And what there was of cricket (with apologies to Mr George Robey) was not good. The day ambled along unprofitably, flat as ditch-water, till at the end one had a vivid sense of the truth of Mr Chesterton's definition of a yawn as a silent yell. England batted first on a good wicket—good despite that now and again a ball " popped " uncomfortably —and in 160 minutes managed to score 129 for four wickets against a more or less mediocre attack.

Only Mailey of the Australian bowlers found his best form. Macdonald and Gregory both were out of

KENNINGTON OVAL

mood. One looked upon the fast medium stuff of these two bowlers—compact to a vast extent of long-hops—and then, recollecting the thunderbolts of the same men at Trent Bridge, murmured " What a falling away, what a dwindling since that action ! " Even the Australian fieldsmen hardly had the original gusto, though one got to this notion not from any actual technical deficiency in the Australian scouting.

It was rather a temperamental lack that one suspected in the Australian side—a spiritual lassitude of which they themselves were probably unaware. To the writer, at any rate, some influence seemed at work changing the purposeful men that made the action at Trent Bridge, sniffing battle in the wind exultantly, into so many workers in rote. It may be the Australians are now become stale, it may be that for them the " ashes " are everything in Test cricket, and that, the ashes once won or lost, the rest is anticlimax. Whatever the cause, the Australians did not burn a living flame; there was not even the glow of an incandescence which might flash into a white light suddenly. One, indeed, looked on and said " Dying fires ! "—the conflagration that has consumed the estates of English cricket seemingly was just going out.

England did no proud things in the circumstances to score 129 for four wickets. The Australian bowling not only was below form; it had to grapple with a slippery ball. Russell and Brown made 24 undistinguished runs for the first wicket and Russell then was given out caught at the wicket. To the writer it looked as if his bat did not touch within a foot of the ball. Russell himself was all astonishment as the umpire's decision went against him in response to a solitary appeal from Oldfield. Ernest Tyldesley shaped for a while like a man playing at a pin's point of a ball with a broomstick. He could not establish contact. As he played with his old " half-cock " stroke he was the living image of doubt. One thought of the gay innings he gave us at Manchester, where he was a very D'Artagnan of cricketers, and one wondered at the mystery of the changefulness of form and style.

Brown again played a brave game. Now and again a ball " kicked " and hit him, but he did not turn a hair. There is a touch of rich nature about this cricketer. The angular and raw aspect of his body, the vivid flesh tints of his high cheek bones cause one vividly to think of some figure in a Ford Madox Brown canvas—say, the man with the spade in " Work." Brown batted for more than seventy minutes, using a nice judgment. Then he suddenly got out of control and made a farmyard stroke at a well-pitched ball from Mailey.

Woolley gave the one touch of style to the English batting. His innings, though fleeting, was charming and quite his own. His bat did not go out to the ball, as Ernest Tyldesley's did, as though it were blind. It was a living bat with a sense for the flight of a ball. The crack of it as it made a stroke sweetly in the middle gave us the happiest music one can hear on the cricket field. Woolley's innings ended sadly.

KENNINGTON OVAL

One saw the breaking of it as one might see a precious vase smashed clumsily to pieces. Woolley cut a ball to third man. At the end of the first run Bardsley picked the ball up on the boundary's edge. Woolley went for another run, but before he could get home Bardsley had thrown in magnificently a distance of some 80 yards and had hit the middle stump. Woolley was strangely lethargic in his movement across the wicket. Possibly he imagined Bardsley would never for a moment dream that here was a chance of running a man out. In English county cricket, true, it is not fashionable to throw a batsman's wicket down from the boundary's edge.

Ernest Tyldesley was on view for one hour and forty minutes and Collins badly missed him in the slips off Gregory when he was 4. Towards the end of his innings he began to " see " the ball, and now and then his bat made dashing play. He never mastered the attack, though, and nobody was astounded at his downfall to a bad stroke on the off side (all uppish hits on the offside are bad). The afternoon fizzled out to some intolerably ugly batting by Mead.

The Oval crowd was big considering the weather, and in the afternoon made for itself a slight sensation. It was no doubt driven to the act by sheer boredom. A heavy shower fell at 2.40 and another at a quarter to four. For a while the crowd waited quietly for some sign that the cricketers had not gone home to bed. At last patience broke down. The multitude moved over the field, and, concentrating in front of the pavilion, demanded cricket. Tennyson spoke from the balcony, stating that if the crowd would retire quietly to the seats, an inspection of the wicket would be made. Whereat the crowd assumed the aspect of your Shakespearean rabble and asked for Armstrong. Armstrong did not come forth. After more hubbub, Tennyson, with the umpires, looked at the wicket, and then a board was carried around the field giving an assurance of play at 5.15. The crowd now returned in perfect order to the seats. The behaviour of the Oval crowd on this Saturday has been harshly written down as unsportsmanlike. Yet the people had some provocation. For nearly an hour they waited in vain for somebody in authority to show himself. Moreover the sun was now shining, and the crowd could see for themselves that the turf was drying rapidly. It is conceivable that the disturbance would not have happened at all had an important law of English cricket been rigidly kept in force throughout the day. In this law we are told " the umpires are sole judges of the fitness of the ground, the weather, the light for play." Moreover instructions to umpires have been issued to this point: " In case of interference from rain, as soon as the rain has ceased the umpires shall immediately, without further instruction, inspect the wicket, unaccompanied by any of the players, and decide upon its fitness."

KENNINGTON OVAL

SECOND DAY, AUGUST 15th, 1921.
(Scores at Close of Play.)

ENGLAND—First Innings.

Brown, b Mailey	32
Russell, c Oldfield, b Macdonald	13
Tyldesley (E.). c Macartney, b Gregory	39
Woolley, run out	23
Mead, not out	182
Sandham, b Macdonald	21
L. H. Tennyson, b Macdonald	51
P. G. Fender, c Armstrong, b Macdonald	0
Hitch, b Macdonald	13
J. W. H. T. Douglas, not out	21
Extras	8
Total (for eight wickets)	403

(Innings declared.) Parkin did not bat.

AUSTRALIA—First Innings.

H. L. Collins, hit wicket, b Hitch	14
W. Bardsley, b Hitch	22
C. G. Macartney, b Douglas	61
T. J. E. Andrews, not out	59
Extras	6
Total (for three wickets)	162

J. M. Taylor, C. E. Pellew, W. W. Armstrong, J. M. Gregory, W. A. Oldfield, E. A. Macdonald, and A. A. Mailey to bat.

In this summer of England's leanness it has happened for one of our batsmen to establish a record for Test cricket in this country. To-day Mead, of Hampshire, has scored 182 not out, and so has improved on W. G. Grace's innings of 170 made in 1886—an innings which till this afternoon has ranked as the highest innings fashioned by a batsman in International games played here. This performance, as Dr Johnson would have called it, of Mead came to greatness by the process of saturation—in Henry

A CRICKETER'S BOOK

James's term. That is to say, it was batsmanship which got impressive through sheer massiveness. Had one seen but a section of the innings—any hour of it—one could hardly have captured from the style and colour of it an impression likely to last a week. But as Mead persisted from hour to hour, his unwearying vigilance, his very solidity, gave one to think that here was a man making history. The innings assumed the majestic manner—passing along the day, ponderous but processional.

Mead batted five hours and scored his runs out of a total of 319. He hit 21 fours and gave but one reasonable catch to the Australian field. That happened when he was 75, and the chance went to Mailey, who dropped a quick cut to the slips. Yesterday the writer spoke of the ugliness of Mead's batsmanship. Now may Mead retort: "Handsome is as handsome does." His batsmanship to-day had a certain freedom—the movements of it suggested to the fancy the movements of the dancing bear in Ravel's suite, "Mother Goose." There is none of the supple wrist play in his work which we associate with good batsmanship; the whole of his body seems to be in constant adjustment and readjustment as he exploits his range of strokes. Yet with all Mead's clumsiness, his hits are actually most cleanly and neatly made. His on-side cricket is astonishingly sure and quick. Also he cuts quite sweetly. Elephantine he is, may be, but like one of the big beasties in the nursery books, he is elephantine with a most likeable agility.

KENNINGTON OVAL

In two hours and a half before lunch the English innings produced 174 runs for the loss of Sandham's wicket, and may be said to have fallen into two periods—pre- and post-Tennysonian. At the morning's outset Sandham and Mead played skilful cricket enough, but their game was tactically incorrect. England's policy now surely demanded forceful measures. Sandham and Mead made 62 runs in an hour—this pedestrian movement on a perfect Oval wicket with two days only to get through, and England so placed that she had everything to gain and little to lose by indulging the wayfarer's courage.

While Mead and Sandham cultivated the academic mood, clouds hung over the field, hinting of rain. Was not England's plan in this moment to pile runs up greedily on the off-chance that a bowler's wicket later in the day would give our bowlers aid to get rid of Australia twice in convenient time? It so turned out that the weather more or less behaved itself, but Sandham and Mead, while they dawdled, could hardly have guaranteed a fine day. Thus the cricket they cultivated together was not particularly helpful to England's purpose. Even with an assurance of fine weather, these batsmen would have had no excuse for slow scoring, since little enough time was now at England's service for the job of running through the Australian batsmen twice. It might be argued that Sandham and Mead were blunting the edge of the Australian attack, but, as a fact, observation of that attack from behind the bowlers' arm revealed that it had little edge on it at any time. Gregory was definitely a second-rate fast-medium man; Mailey could not get a length; Armstrong had a length, true, but no spin. Only Macdonald looked like a Test match bowler. He even performed, time after time, the miracle of a break-back on that flawless turf. But more often than not he pitched it so short that the batsmen could watch it comfortably. Sandham was bowled by one of these break-backs, exactly at twelve o'clock. He has a nice upright style, and perhaps the fact that he was in his first Test match prevented him to some extent from playing a really useful game for England.

England's right policy was put beautifully into force immediately after the advent of Tennyson. Not only did Tennyson himself flash an adventuresome bat at the bowling; he even cast animation upon Mead. All the morning Mead had batted with the surest judgment, and looked to possess an impregnable defence. But he needed for the making of his first fifty not less than one hour and fifty-five minutes. Even with Tennyson in, Mead at first did not bestir himself. Then at last Tennyson had words with him in mid-wicket. One could not, of course, be sure of the purport of these words, but from subsequent events one could guess. At any rate, Mead went back to his crease after the conversation a changed man. The very next two balls he had to face were hit to the boundary—and Armstrong himself was the bowler.

Now, the English innings went along at a fine and politic speed. Tennyson, if he did not recapture his

KENNINGTON OVAL

Leeds mastery, at least punched hard any loose ball. Mead, as one has suggested, assumed the aspect of greatness through his gathering energy. He moved to his second fifty in some seventy minutes. Tennyson and Mead added 121 for the sixth wicket in 100 minutes. During this stand the Australian bowling went totally to pieces. One asked pensively whether batsmen like Mead and Tennyson would have discovered Gregory and Macdonald's fallibility even at Trent Bridge. There is no answer to the question. This day's cricket provides no clue, at any rate, for these Australians were not the Joves of Trent Bridge. Yet satisfaction comes to us from the English batsmanship to-day: we are in a position to argue that against resolute men like the Mead of this match Gregory and Macdonald might conceivably have been made to look perfectly human and liable to error—even at Trent Bridge.

The English innings was declared just on 4 o'clock. Only Hitch, after Tennyson was out, assisted Mead at the wise game for England. Douglas batted a quarter of an hour without opening his score, improving neither England's prospects nor his reputation. After lunch Gregory and Macdonald bowled for one hour and thirty-five minutes unchanged. Mailey hurt his hand trying to catch Mead from a hard return, and after the interval he could not bowl.

Australia's innings started at a quarter-past four, and straightway Hitch found a rare pace—faster than Durston's or Howell's. He clean bowled Bardsley with a capital break-back, with Australia's score 33.

A CRICKETER'S BOOK

Then the English field threw away heaven-sent opportunities. Macartney was missed, his score only two, by Woolley in the slips; Collins also gave a catch at the wicket which Brown dropped. England might well have had Australia's three best batsmen out for a mere 50. Hitch now dwindled in speed, and there was no other England bowler with bite in him. Douglas and Fender between them probably sent down more half-volleys and long-hops in half-an-hour than Attewell and Shaw bowled in their lifetimes. Macartney and Andrews both were bad starters, but they settled down in time to a confident and polished game. The English fielding was hardly trustworthy: Parkin at cover-point did as well as anybody. "Always put your bowler at cover if possible," commented a wag in the pavilion.

LAST DAY, AUGUST 16th, 1921.
(Final Scores.)

ENGLAND—First Innings.

Russell, c Oldfield, b Macdonald	13
Brown, b Mailey	32
Tyldesley (E.), c Macartney, b Gregory	39
Woolley (F. E.), run out	23
Mead, not out	182
Sandham, b Macdonald	21
L. H. Tennyson, b Macdonald	51
P. G. Fender, c Armstrong, b Macdonald	0
Hitch, b Macdonald	18
J. W. H. T. Douglas, not out	21
Extras	3
Total (for eight wickets)	403

(Innings declared closed.) Parkin did not bat.

KENNINGTON OVAL

Australia—First Innings.

H. L. Collins, hit wicket, b Hitch	14
W. Bardsley, b Hitch	22
C. G. Macartney, b Douglas	61
T. J. E. Andrews, lbw, b Parkin	94
J. M. Taylor, c Woolley, b Douglas	75
C. E. Pellew, c Woolley, b Parkin	1
W. W. Armstrong, c Brown, b Douglas	19
J. M. Gregory, st Brown, b Parkin	27
W. A. Oldfield, not out	28
E. A. Macdonald, st Brown, b Woolley	86
A. A. Mailey, b Woolley	0
Extras	12
Total	389

England—Second Innings.

Russell, not out	102
Brown, c Mailey, b Taylor	84
P. G. Fender, c Armstrong, b Mailey	6
Hitch, not out	51
Extra	1
Total (for two wickets)	244

Australian Bowling—First Innings.

	O.	M.	R.	W.		O.	M.	R.	W.
Gregory	38	5	128	1	Mailey	30	4	85	1
Macdonald	47	9	143	5	Armstrong	12	2	44	0

Second Innings.

	O.	M.	R.	W.		O.	M.	R.	W.
Gregory	3	0	13	0	Andrews	8	0	44	0
Macdonald	6	0	20	0	Taylor	7	1	25	1
Mailey	18	2	77	1	Collins	7	0	39	0
Pellew	9	3	25	0					

England Bowling—First Innings.

	O.	M.	R.	W.		O.	M.	R.	W.
Hitch	19	3	65	2	Parkin	23	4	82	3
Douglas	30	2	117	3	Woolley	11	2	31	2
Fender	19	3	82	0					

There was little interest remaining in the last Test match when the cricketers went into the sunny field this morning, and that little interest passed away as soon as Andrews and Taylor set to work. Both batsmen played the most confident and easeful cricket imaginable. Straightway one understood that the miracle of English bowling needed to whisk the match into the air of high drama was not to happen.

The cricket would have had its charm, with the scene of it some rustic meadow and the players just hearty yeomen like the players in " Evan Harrington." In such happy circumstances one most gratefully would have sprawled on the grass, watching the movements of the men in white through the mellow haze, fully content with these simple things. But Test cricket must be competitive else it is nothing; its setting allows of no summer amenities. So to-day the spirit of the game suffered a blight. Interest in the play was of necessity strictly academic. At the afternoon's fall, cheap distinction came to English batsmen—Taylor, Andrews, and Pellew bowling at them—but nobody, not even the crowd, took this phase of the match seriously.

In the opening quarter of an hour of the day Australia's score jumped from 162 to 192. Hitch and Douglas bowled—and Douglas bowled wretchedly. Yet he was permitted to send four overs along for 26 runs. A few of the hits from his bowling were generously fielded by Parkin somewhere near coverpoint. Not till Parkin was asked to take a share in the English attack at 215 did the Australian pace of scoring flag. And Parkin it was that upset the Andrews-Taylor partnership, after it had made 71

KENNINGTON OVAL

runs in forty-five minutes. In Parkin's next over he overthrew Pellew. This capital bowling, however, seemingly did not impinge on the mind of Tennyson, who to the end of the Australian innings persistently used Parkin definitely as a change bowler. But of this a little more later.

The innings of Andrews can perhaps be written down in the highest class. His batsmanship had lustre. He was ever attacking the bowling—even as he came close upon his first Test match century; he was ever moving in fine animation along a fruitful way. He produced all the authentic scoring strokes, giving them an outline of rare clarity. The purity and boldness of what one might call th contours of his innings permitted one to describe it Pre-Raphaelitish. His footwork had the dancing master's swiftness and economy. He was in position in nice time for his strokes and seemingly executed them with the slightest body energy. His cover drives might well have contained in them nothing but the propulsion of his wrists. If he once lifted a ball in the air the writer did not notice it. The disposition of his body in all his strokes was so classically correct that an uppish stroke seemed impossible from him. It was orthodox batsmanship maybe, but certainly not dull. Andrews batted two hours, and hit eleven fours. Andrews is thirty-one years old, and so he has time to develop into a second Sidney Gregory, whose mantle he has plainly in his keeping.

Of the rest of the Australians' innings only Taylor's innings invites comment. He played an impudent

A CRICKETER'S BOOK

but brilliant game in making his first fifty, then dwindled to dullness. Taylor's drives were of uncommon power, this despite that he seemed to make them with his weight on the back foot. He obviously uses forearm leverage. Australia's score at lunch was 338 for seven, and on taking up the game after the interval Gregory and Oldfield unmistakably were out for an Australian first innings win. But Parkin dismissed Gregory at once—and his reward for this bowling feat was relegation again to a position in the off side field. With the hitter Macdonald in, alongside Oldfield, Tennyson did his best, though, of course, unwittingly, to present Armstrong with first innings' laurels. For Tennyson's management of his bowling now became utterly wrong-headed. He did not allow his fast bowler, Hitch, to get at the rabbits —according to the custom of cricket captains like MacLaren and Darling. Instead he asked the innocuous Fender to bowl, and Woolley. Thus the ninth Australian wicket added fifty-one runs in forty minutes. As events turned out Woolley took the ninth and tenth wickets, finishing the Australian innings at 389. None the less, with Parkin and Hitch on the field, a slow left-hand bowler against a hitting batsman at this stage of the game was indiscreet tactics. Macdonald drove powerfully to the on side, and once Sandham caught him magnificently on the boundary edge, but the hit came from a no-ball. Later Macdonald sent another drive, this time from a lawful ball, and though the catch was easier than the other, Sandham dropped it.

KENNINGTON OVAL

The match fizzled out when England went in again at half-past three, though the crowd stayed on in the comfortable sunshine. They had the rare delectation of witnessing Armstrong field in the country. Armstrong, if he felt any secret pathos as the lovely afternoon passed on, taking him to the end of his Test match career, cleverly disguised it. He was all affability, like the man in Mr Jacobs's novel.

England probably had in all the match but one chance of winning it. That was when Macartney gave the slip chance to Woolley. Yet it was really always a remote prospect that on this glorious Oval wicket a batting side like Australia would be overthrown twice in a day and a half. The issue conceivably might have been tighter had Tennyson deployed his bowling cleverly. He persistently regarded Parkin as a change bowler. He even allowed Parkin to bowl only four overs more than Fender. The contrast in quality of these two bowlers' work is not even fully indicated by the bowling analysis. Fender possibly bowled as badly as ever cricketer was permitted to bowl in Test cricket. Tennyson's leadership was also at fault on Monday evening, when, in a declining light, he asked Hitch to bowl with the sightscreen behind him instead of from the pavilion end. If Tennyson was possessed by any delicacy towards the Australians on this tactical point, then he was surely wasting it on Armstrong, who goes into action with no soft gloves on.

PART III
OF AUSTRALIANS

"Eleven buckram men."

CHAPTER I

ARMSTRONG AND THE AUSTRALIAN GAME

(*May* 1921)

ARMSTRONG is the Australian all over. If a sculptor —and he would need to be a rough-hewing Rodin— wished to make a figure that might be representative of cricket as it is played in Australia, no better model than the Australian captain could he find. Australian cricket is incarnate in Armstrong as he walks from the pavilion, bat in hand—" he that to bar the first gate doth as wide as the great Rhodian Colossus stride." Consider the man's huge bulk when, crouching just a little, he faces the bowler. He bespeaks vigilance, suspicion, determination. Your Australian is a Spartan every inch; to achieve conquest he will scourge himself if needs be. For him it is victory or nothing. No savour in cricket for an Armstrong if Australia lose.

This complete submission of self to the will to conquer is not always a mark of the English game. We have inclined in recent years to seek for something more in cricket than the spoils of battle, something more than a combat which, if it bring not victory, turns all in the mouth to dust. What Lancashire cricket lover would have had his team triumphant over Sussex a few years ago at the cost of a century by Ranjitsinhji? There was a famous Saturday at Old Trafford, upon which thousands of men and women, who loved a Lancashire victory right well, groaned out their disappointment unashamedly as they saw Ranji dismissed for a mere song by a Lancashire bowler. We have made an art out of cricket in this country; we like to see the unfolding of personality, and, indeed, we fall now and again so entranced under the sway of art for art's sake—in other words, batsmanship for its pure loveliness—that we forget for the while which way the battle goes. So, too, with some of our cricketers. For your Hobbs, your Woolley, your Spooner, your J. T. Tyldesley, cricket's cardinal sin is to be untrue to oneself and the style that is the man, whatever the occasion. Hobbs, in the hour of England's defeat at Sydney the other winter, scored, so the cables told us, "with all his own ease." He was bowled in an endeavour to flick a ball from the leg stump to the boundary. The artist all over and, if you like, his egoism! Not for Hobbs the prosaic way—only by his own adventurous paths can he take his side to victory.

This must seem to a man like Armstrong a philosophy of vanity. The clannish Australian conception of a game has no room in it for a spreading of peacock feathers. For Armstrong the team, and not any one man in it, is the cue to action. The motive power of a great Australian eleven is collective effort; it is a machine functioning towards vic-

ARMSTRONG AND THE AUSTRALIAN GAME

tory, and there is small room in its grinding remorselessness for the man prone to fall in love with a mere æsthetic contemplation of cricket. Not that Australia has never had her artist-cricketers. There was Trumper, who would flash his bat at disaster, and at the end cry " Vixi! " And to-day Australia has Macartney, as thrilling and as arrogant in egoism as Ranji himself. But here we have genius transcending the type. Armstrong is truer to the Australian spirit.

The Australian appetite for victory tends, as we have seen, to make mere fighting machines of cricketers, no matter how much of character they may possess individually. But there is another point which might be used to explain the large predominance in Australian cricket of one type. In Australia, identical conditions obtain in nineteen matches out of twenty—hard turf, a white light. Is it astonishing then that technique tends to get standardised? The Australian cricketer is fashioned in a mould; continuity of environment means continuity of type. How different from this the making of English cricketers. We have a variable climate, and, as a consequence, a variable technique. A man is at Lord's one day in sunshine on a turf of lightning pace—to-morrow he is in the mud and mire at Bramall Lane. Diversity of setting assists towards diversity of style. These material factors alone, leaving out differences of temperament, would explain the collectivism of Australian cricket and the individualism of English cricket.

Armstrong's batsmanship is ever expressing the dour attitude of mind behind the Australian game. His poise at the crease has no hint of the joyous abandon of Trumper. No; Armstrong, as he gets down to his work, steels himself for the ordeal by battle—a battle with " No quarter! " the cry in his ranks. None of your amenities for Armstrong—on the field, at least. He that has no stomach to this fight let him depart, is his doctrine. What pitiless acts of self-abnegation the man will suffer that Australia might win—or not be beaten. In 1905, at Nottingham Darling found all his bowlers, save Armstrong, out of form. He decided, therefore, that if Australia could not win she must at all costs frustrate England's chances. A drawn game was his object, almost from the outset of the match. And towards this grim purpose he instructed Armstrong to bowl outside the leg stump, with his field packed on that side, the object, of course, being to prevent England from making the number of runs necessary for victory. The point I wish to stress here is that Armstrong surely had some reason for supposing that by bowling at the wicket he could get a few men out. But the captain had spoken. Armstrong cast personal vanity aside, and for a whole afternoon became a sheer bowling automaton, pitching the ball to a halfpenny's circumference wide of the leg wicket, heedless of the crowd's jeers and of MacLaren's irony, until he had bowled 52 overs, 24 maidens, for 67 runs. This is the toll on egoism taken by

ARMSTRONG AND THE AUSTRALIAN GAME

the Australian conception of cricket as sheer combat!

And it is a philosophy likely enough to prevail. The Australian game is not as attractive as ours, but it is hardier. Armstrong's batsmanship has a quite cruel sort of toughness. He forces the ball in front of the wicket with more violence than any other man in cricket to-day. And as he swings his enormous shoulders, we get no hint of abandon, or joyful sense of physical mastery. Rather does this colossal energy suggest a giant using his power because he must—because if he force not home the advantage he will perish. Not a graceful batsman—" Pah! what is grace, and how much is it worth?" we can imagine him asking—but he is thrilling to watch all the same. He does not give us the poetry of batsmanship as Victor Trumper did. Yet this is perhaps not quite true. There is nothing of mere prose about Armstrong. If he does not get his runs with the rhymed gracefulness of a Trumper, he at least gives us the blank verse of batsmanship, so to speak, and there is a powerful rhythm in it.

CHAPTER II

GREGORY

(*August* 1921)

THE idea one got of the Australians when first they came to us remains well in mind yet. One saw them in action for the first time in the nets at Lord's as a soft spring day went to its close, and one's impression of the afternoon is still of tonic air and loveliness of fresh green grass, with keen young men in tune with the nipping season of the year. They had the bronze of the Australian sun on their faces; they gave out the radiance of well-being. And now the season is over one feels that it was the sting of youth that moved the Australians to their great conquests. Cleverer Australian teams have visited us, but none quite so fresh, so eager as this. Who will forget the new-born vigour and impulsiveness of Gregory as he bowled down our wickets at Trent Bridge? Who will forget the winged feet of Pellew, the lissome agility of Andrews and Hendry? If ever brilliant fielding won matches it was during this Australian tour. The mature cricketers on the side made their notable contribution from day to day, but it is the young men we shall think upon the longest.

Gregory lost his energy after the third Test match

at Leeds. Though he had a moment or so of triumph at Old Trafford against Lancashire, he was not the irresistible Gregory Trent Bridge saw, and in the fourth Test match at Manchester he was just a caricature of himself. Gregory went to pieces as soon as the rubber was safe in Armstrong's keeping. It is said that half-through the season his knee began to give him trouble. Without mention of a physical handicap, though, it would be possible, one thinks, to account for Gregory's dwindling once the ashes were Australia's. He always looked a bowler for a " psychological moment "; his greatest moments (so it struck the writer) came when the issue provided a spur to effort beyond his common capacity. For Gregory at his best did not seem an easeful bowler, or even a spontaneous bowler. He had the air that he got his great pace by sheer will-power. Though his action had a most thrilling beauty, it was like the beauty of some proud ship ploughing heavy waters. There was not Macdonald's smooth-running mechanism in Gregory's action. It is possible to argue, then, that as soon as the main incentive—that is, the winning of the rubber—went out of the tour, Gregory slackened power. This does not necessarily mean that Gregory consciously bowled with a slighter effort than before. No doubt he tried as hard as ever in the fourth Test at Manchester, where his bowling was hardly to be recognised as Gregory's. The pressure of events works subtly on a man, and he is often the last person in the world to feel conscious of the influences that move him to his strongest endeavour.

Gregory, time after time, even in the earlier Test matches, when a constant incentive to his biggest efforts was before him, proved himself a cricketer definitely susceptible to an " occasion." At Lord's, for instance, in the second Test match, England looked like pulling themselves out of a nasty hole on the second day. Douglas and Woolley were well set and England's score round about 120 for three. With seven wickets in hand England was beginning to draw ahead of Australia. Armstrong now put his ambling geniality aside and asked for a special effort from his fast bowlers. Straightway Gregory answered his cue and bowled Douglas with a break-back worthy of Richardson. Technically Macdonald was always Gregory's better. But technique is not everything. Gregory was the stouter-hearted bowler. The will to victory worked in him strongest in those moments when victory looked hardest to win. One has indeed rarely seen a cricketer who carried himself, at his best, so persistently like a man on a winning side as Gregory. He had youth's own confidence—and how very much it means to a bowler, if he can always tackle a batsman firmly believing he is the better man ! In the first three Test matches Gregory looked to the writer like a man burning a white flame of confidence. His onrush to the wicket and the fierce energy of his final leap were a quite strident announcement of the joy of youth and power.

Justice has not been done to Gregory's bowling in the critical Test matches. Even good judges of the game go on repeating the parrot-cry about Gregory's

GREGORY

bumping ball and the danger of it to life and limb. Yet no less acute an observer of cricket than A. C. MacLaren has stated that Gregory's bowling in the first half-hour of the first Test match at Trent Bridge was compact of half-volleys. My own impression of Gregory's work in this period is that he bowled not one short ball, a few half-volleys, and far too many superbly pitched and tremendously fast break-backs for England's liking! It was fast bowling the terrific quality of which I had not seen since the best days of Neville Knox. From a position almost in line behind the wicket I could see the ball pitch outside the off stump and whip back gloriously. The ball that upset Hendren's wicket Lockwood himself would have been proud to own. To suggest that the English batsman in that awful opening half-hour at Trent Bridge lost their wickets to half-volleys through lack of heart is untrue, as a glance at Gregory's bowling analysis may help to show. Here it is:—

.	.	2	.	.	.	.	.	1	.
1	.	.	.	.	w	.	.	.	1
4	4	1	.	.	w	w	.	2	2

It will be seen that from Gregory's first over nine runs were hit, including two boundaries. Loose balls were hit stoutly enough when Gregory bowled them. Is it likely that Holmes and Knight were panic-stricken after so heartening a beginning? Let justice be done to Gregory. He beat his batsman skill for skill—and the batsmen themselves will tell you as much.

A CRICKETER'S BOOK

The beauty of Gregory's break-back in the opening matches of the Australian tour seems to have escaped a lot of critics. Little reference was made to it, and in conversations about Gregory to-day you will hear scant allusion to it. The fact is, only a few spectators in a cricket crowd are in a position to watch the direction of a ball—everybody can't find room behind the bowler's arm. And the press boxes on most county grounds are placed at an angle to the wicket which prevents close scrutiny of a bowler's art. That is one reason why criticism is commonly better informed upon batsmanship than it is upon bowling. A Ranji can be admired from any position on the ground. Gregory's break-back first came to the notice of the writer at Lord's during the net practice in April, and in his notebook he wrote this paragraph: " He did not, of course, bowl his fastest in the nets, but he sent the ball along full of life, and there was a suggestion of superb latent power in his action. More sinister still, he occasionally broke back some four inches. If Gregory can reproduce that off-break this summer in conjunction with his authentic pace, then the ashes will remain just where they are to-day." That Gregory did reproduce the break-back at his best pace in the critical Test matches will not be denied by Hendren, at any rate, whoever else is sceptical. It was not, of course, a break-back got by finger spin. The break came from body action. Gregory, like Richardson, flung the upper part of his body over the left leg to the off side as the arm came over, the fingers sweeping under the ball as it left his hand. The ball was propelled in this way rather to the off side, and on pitching bounced rather than broke back. There was little subtlety in his bowling. He had few resources. But at his best he had one magnificent trick—and it served.

CHAPTER III

BARDSLEY AND MACARTNEY

ONE criticism of the Australians common enough throughout their conquering summer was rather naive: " Where would they be as a batting side without Bardsley and Macartney ? " As well might one ask where would " Othello " be as a play without Iago and the Moor. The fact our bowlers had to face was that the Australians were never without Bardsley and Macartney—on important occasions, and that these two great batsmen came along, more often than not, with bats full of runs. And the suggestion that lacking Bardsley and Macartney the Australians would have been easy game for our bowlers is not supported by the Test match records. There were five Australian batsmen, apart from the two masters, whose averages were higher than 25 an innings.

But the calibre of the Australian batting is not to be explained by a reference to averages. The great point about it was that for the uses of cricket played against the clock, it was much more likely to win matches than our own. One might have expected to find the Australians less successful than English batsmen at the forcing tactics needful in three-day cricket, seeing that in their own country

BARDSLEY AND MACARTNEY

matches are conducted without cognisance of time, to a quite "heavenly length."

It was, as a fact, the Englishmen, not the Australians, who went in to bat believing that for the first half-hour at the wicket runs did not matter, and that those canny preliminaries known as "playing oneself in" could be safely cultivated.

An Australian batsman put it to the writer, after the fifth Test match, in these terms: "In a three-day match you can't afford to waste time playing yourself in. At any rate, it is bad cricket to get so absorbed in the job that you overlook the half-volleys. A good cricketer ought in all circumstances to hit the first ball he gets for four if it is a bad one, but the Englishman rarely 'lets go' at the rankest length stuff until he has been in the middle a longish time." The Australian batsmanship was plastic, aggressive or dogged as circumstances demanded, ever keen on "the main chance"; ours had little opportunism in it,—taking the same course, in spirit and method, whether the game swung in England's favour, as it did at the Oval and at Manchester, or whether it went dead against us, as it most unhappily did for the best part of the Tests.

The Australian batting was not variable in style. Apart from Macartney and Bardsley there were no "individualists"; the bulk of them, though they got runs briskly, played a typical Australian game, one clearly the product of practice in a land of hard wickets. The type was transcended by Macartney and Bardsley, whose work told you definitely something about the men themselves. Their cricket had art in the truest sense; it expressed personality. To see them together in a big partnership was to have a complete introduction to batsmanship. So contrasted were the methods of them that one was forcibly made to reflect that in all human activity extreme ability develops in two divergent ways, according to temperament, making of men either liberals or conservatives, classics or romantics.

Bardsley was orthodox, true to the ancient faith, a batsman who scrupulously observed the principles which long experience has sanctioned. Macartney was the heretic, reckless of the " unities," flashing an audacious bat in his own way. " Dignity and Impudence," said one, watching them at the wicket. Bardsley appealed to our respect for law and order and tradition; Macartney appealed to the rebel that is in each of us, to one's deep-rooted hankering after the mischievous. There was an Olympian contentment in Bardsley's play: for him batsmanship as the old masters knew it was good enough—batsmanship in love with its own chaste outlines. He played like one willing to pass along the old tranquil ways for ever: his was cricket quite without desire, fit for heaven and eternity. But into the batting of Macartney the modern spirit of unrest entered. He chafed at the limits which a chiselled perfection like Bardsley's puts upon batsmanship. For him an innings was always a great adventure. Bardsley's cricket might have moved to the serene and contented rhythm of the music which is known as Handel's Largo, but Macartney's called for wild and whirring music, some impudent scherzo, and Dukas's "L'Apprenti Sorcier" would have done. The writer, indeed, rarely saw Macartney bat without thinking of Dukas's mad masterpiece. For did not Macartney in truth use his bat as some apprentice in magic might mischievously use his master's wand, weaving spells gaily, but unaware that in his charge was the power to achieve sheer destruction? He conjured the ball to the boundary with a cross bat, cutting it dead from the middle stump. But sometimes the magic tricked even Macartney and down went the middle stump. Perhaps, though, he was too masterful for the simile of the sorcerer's apprentice to fit. Rather did he suggest at times, a practised wizard a little tired of his own trickery—tired through too much familiarity with the marvellous. One great innings by Macartney, at Leicester, had cynicism's own note in it; this was the cricket of a master disillusioned. "I am tired of conquest," he seemed to say, "satiated with boundaries that are cheap. I sigh for new worlds for my art to conquer —and there is none!"

The rest of the Australian batting, as one has suggested, had a collective rather than individual quality. Andrews, Collins, Pellew, Gregory, Armstrong, and Taylor in the mass ensured formidable run-getting powers. Compare them individually with, say, Russell, Brown, Douglas, Mead, Tennyson, and Tyldesley (England's best batsmen, after Woolley and Hearne—who, roughly, may be written down as the equivalents of Bardsley and Macartney) and the Englishmen would seem in every instance to have the advantage in skill. But the Australians cultivoted the team spirit intelligently, and every man of them came out pounds stronger in the lump than he would have done playing " on his own." Save for one innings at Leeds, where he used his bat like a hammer, Armstrong in the Tests did not make runs like a master. Andrews was the best batsman on the side—after the two geniuses. He improved vastly as the season went on, and at the Oval his cricket had the sting of style in it. Taylor will surely train on to mastership. At present he is a genius in the making, trying to use the technique of the fully-fledged genius. He would do well to lean for a while on the stout first principles of his fathers. Even Macartney studied in an orthodox school, mastering the ancient laws before daring to shatter them.

Armstrong had so much batting at hand that he could go through the Test matches without once calling on Mayne and Ryder, both of them first-class batsmen. Mayne could hardly have hoped for a chance in the big games, because he is so obviously not capable of Australian fielding form. But Ryder had reason to consider himself unlucky. He was in all the Test matches in Australia last winter and played usefully. He is not a good outfield, but near the wicket we have Fender's testimony that he is now and again brilliant. In the season Ryder scored 1,032 runs, averaging 38 an innings. He was distinctly a useful batsman, not inspired, maybe, but one capable of piling up a mass of runs in a dry summer simply by working so many hours a day—much as Anthony Trollope wrote some of his novels.

CHAPTER IV

IMPRESSIONS FROM LORD'S

(*June* 1921)

For the Test match manner Lord's is very becoming. Last week's big game played anywhere, no doubt would have left some fine memories. But because it all happened at Lord's the sense of greatness comes into one's impressions. The momentous is in the air at Lord's; the place is murmurous with history. Any great occasion there merges into the greater past, even as it goes on in front of us. Splendour from other days descended on last week's Test, and cricketers of to-morrow will speak well of it. They will tell one another that Woolleys are now no more, that once on a time an Armstrong bestrode the field.

It was a match with its little tragedies. Hendren missed his footing on the upper slopes of greatness, and to-day he is rather fallen. This time last summer few of us had a hint that he was not one of the masters. He is perceptibly diminished now. D. J. Knight had an unhappy match also. Those who saw the expression on his face as he came back to the pavilion on Monday, out to a dreadful stroke for a single, will not quickly forget its wistfulness. The President of the Immortals has surely had his hour of

IMPRESSIONS FROM LORD'S

sport over Knight—endowing him in the beginning with every grace a cricketer could desire, but withholding the touchstone Luck. As Knight walked sadly back to the Lord's pavilion last week—taking off his batting gloves with the air of one knowing only too well that not for a long time was he likely to put them on again for England—did the remembrance of his experience at Trent Bridge prick him with irony? For in England's second innings at Trent Bridge, Knight had his period of proud batsmanship. He assumed the aspect of a master cricketer and made 38 like any Spooner. And then with Test match laurels in his very grasp they were snatched abominably away; Hendren ran him out. The President of the Immortals allowed Knight to spread wings and to soar a little, then brought him to earth with a cruel bolt. We all know that Knight is a batsman. Did Hendren's unhappy accident cut short a season of plenty? Had Knight gone on for an hour at Trent Bridge—and he was all confidence and mastery while he was in—might not the future have been secure for him, might not a great innings have put him along the confident way? Life has its little ironies in cricket that are not less mordant than the Wessex brand.

But the match at Lord's was not all tragedy—at least, not for Australia. The comfortable humours of man are not to be chilled where Armstrong goes his ways. What a piece of loose rotundity he is, what juicy humanity is in him! Someone has called him a cricketing Falstaff. The simile will not do. There is no kind of alacrity about Armstrong, no apprehensiveness, nothing forgetive. Nor is quick wit a part of him. His composition is of humours, shrewd instincts, and most likeable flesh. Australia has never sent us a captain that came closer to English companionship. He is the great figure in the Eleven, though there are others that have the sting of style in their very presence. Macartney, a quick sparrow of a man, his eyes pin-points of alertness and always quizzing you! And there is Pellew affecting one lyrically and no less, as he passes along the boundary's edge, all motion, with no ponderable matter in him at all to be moved.

Your matter-of-fact cricketer, though, may have little patience with these mere " dramatic values." He is for practical points touching the combative issue. How lies the wind now, after Lord's, is the question for him; is victory to be sniffed in it? Well, the last Test match had at least two periods in which England did not look like a beaten team. On Monday morning Australia's wickets were falling much too precipitately for Armstrong, and on Monday afternoon it happened for an hour or so that his untamed fast bowlers were whipped. These miracles have been witnessed once, they may come about again. Yet it must be borne in mind that the two periods just mentioned wherein England took courage, had their aftermaths which were ruinous to England. Our bowling on Monday morning was " collared " by the last Australian wicket, and just at the very moment Woolley and Dipper looked like

IMPRESSIONS FROM LORD'S

pulling the game round for us, Gregory and Macdonald discovered new energy. To say the truth, it is not easy to imagine Gregory and Macdonald both out of action for long. Armstrong nurses his fast bowlers wisely. When one of them tires the other carries on; the while Gregory is in the slips taking large quantities of recuperative air into his lungs Macdonald keeps the pace swift and dangerous. Macdonald, indeed, is the better bowler, considering his work day by day. His action is a beautiful example of energy conserved, and so exquisitely rhythmical is it that it seems incapable of producing a feeble ball. Gregory is a man of moods. At three o'clock he might be a mere bull at a gate, sheer brute strength striving to render the long hop deadly. At four o'clock—especially if Armstrong sternly presses him for "an effort"—he takes on the style of a classical fast bowler, with a Nijinsky leap at the wicket, length immaculate, and the body-break of Richardson. All that is in Hobbs of resolution and skill will be needed to keep Macdonald and Gregory at bay for a convenient passage of time. Then there is Mailey, a bowler specially designed for "rabbits."

There is, in truth, no running away from the facts. Woolley, Tennyson, and Dipper hit the Australian bowling boldly and had luck while they were doing it, yet Gregory and Macdonald quickly prevailed again the moment Armstrong gave the cue. Last week's Lord's XI. can, of course, be improved upon, on paper. The next England XI. must have at least two more tough batsmen besides Hobbs and Hearne

A CRICKETER'S BOOK

—cricketers that have experience in big matches. One wonders if the Selection Committee are aware of the resentment that passed over the land when it was known that Holmes and Rhodes had been dropped? One wonders, too, if the Selection Committee are alive to the distrust amongst cricketers of Douglas as a captain? If no better amateur than Douglas can be found for the job, what of Hobbs, Rhodes, or even Strudwick? But, of course, the mere suggestion that an England XI. might be led into the field by a professional cricketer will be regarded as an unholy heresy at Lord's.

CHAPTER V

THE DEFEAT AT EASTBOURNE

(*August* 1921)

FROM the pains which entered the body of English cricket at Trent Bridge in May the good Lord has at long last delivered us. This afternoon, on the sunny Saffrons cricket field, the Australians' colours have been hauled down; the mighty men that authentic England elevens have found unconquerable in ten successive Test matches have been beaten, beaten by a fictitious England eleven under the leadership of our greatest cricket captain, and, moreover, beaten by a side that was routed in a first innings for forty-three paltry runs. Who on Saturday could have got the faintest glimpse of such an end to the match, even in the wildest flight of fancy? All cricketers know well the infinite changefulness of the great game, but to overthrow the might of Australia from no better base than a first innings total of 43—why, the miraculous is here, black magic, the very imps of mischief. There were the most thrilling fluctuations in the day's play; now the game was safe in Armstrong's keeping, now it slipped from his grasp, now, by a desperate motion of the will, Armstrong clutched it again, and then, as, indeed, it looked his for good, out it slipped and MacLaren and his men stuck greedily to it.

A CRICKETER'S BOOK

At the morning's outset Bardsley and Carter played the bowling comfortably. Gibson was seemingly harmless, and from his first three overs 16 runs came. Would other English captains have taken Gibson off after so bad a beginning? MacLaren did not—and true, he had no great amount of bowling at hand to embarrass him. But MacLaren has had faith in Gibson throughout the summer, and to-day the young University cricketer was to justify, as Barnes and Dean once justified, the insight of the master. With Australia's score 52 Gibson clean bowled Bardsley by a glorious ball that pitched on the off stump and hit the leg. Falcon then bowled a fast short one to Carter, who cut it powerfully. In the Test matches such a stroke from an Australian invariably went to the boundary. To-day young Claude Ashton was in the slips; he saw the ball as a swallow sees a fly, darted forward, and caught it magnificently. Now the outlook for Australia was darkening, but soon the confidence of Macartney's and Andrew's cricket made slight sunshine for Armstrong. And with the total 73, Falcon bowled Macartney, who produced a weird stroke with a cross bat. Pellew and Andrews added just 30 for the fifth Australian wicket, which fell when Hubert Ashton brilliantly caught Pellew at slip. So to lunch with no man's appetite keen for food. Australia needed now 87, with five wickets in hand.

Half-an-hour's play after the interval, and surely the victory was Armstrong's entirely. Andrews and Ryder scored 34 runs in this short space, and, worst of all for MacLaren's prospects, they hit Falcon's

THE DEFEAT AT EASTBOURNE

bowling all over the field. The score was 140 for five when MacLaren asked Faulkner to bowl in place of Falcon. The move was made at the last moment, still at the right moment. Gibson broke the Ryder-Andrews partnership at last, but it was Faulkner, in his third over, that placed the Australians completely against the wall by upsetting Andrews's off stump with an excellent ball which whipped across the wicket from leg. Andrews was eighth out at 158, with but 48 wanted now for his side's victory. He was in such fine form that had he endured another fifteen minutes, especially against Falcon, he would most certainly have won the match. Armstrong was the last hope of his team. Was it just MacLaren's good luck, or was it MacLaren's superb knowledge of cricketers that ordained that Faulkner should be bowling when Armstrong came to the wicket? For Armstrong never has been able to cope with Faulkner. To-day he was sorely troubled by the South African's " googly." He used all his cunning to avoid Faulkner, but he had to face the music at last. And Faulkner pitched him a ball whizzing with spin on the leg stump. Armstrong lost it hopelessly, and the ball would have hit the off wicket but for Armstrong's obstructing pad. Faulkner shook the skies with a triumphant " How's that? " and Armstrong had to go. Macdonald and Mailey added nine more or less nondescript runs for the last wicket, which fell to Gibson, and rightly so. He bowled beautifully without a rest throughout the Australian innings. He has a ball which is a good imitation of

Barnes's famous ball, the one that pitches on the leg stump and swings away to the off. He stuck to his task gallantly, and never allowed the crisis to upset him. In the very throes of the crisis Faulkner exploited his finger spin audaciously.

At the finish, Armstrong, in a speech to the jubilant crowd, said his men had been beaten by the better side. It is certain that England in the Test matches could not show the superb fielding, the skilful and intelligent bowling of this side of MacLaren's. The fielding indeed was up to Australian standards. The crowd roared for MacLaren at the close, but MacLaren was rather overcome with emotion, and through a deputy announced this was his farewell to cricket. A beautiful farewell it has been, putting the crown on his greatness. Not in his hey-day did he give us finer captaincy than he has given us in this match. It was plain this afternoon that his very presence in the field gave his men hope and courage.

Let nobody get the impression that the Australians flung this game away through a casual attitude towards it. Possibly there was just half-an-hour of negligent batsmanship when the Australians went in against a total of 43. But from the fall of Collins's wicket on Saturday, Armstrong had his men strung taut enough. And this afternoon Armstrong's face as he witnessed the breaking of Andrews's wicket—which was a certain omen of the end—had a profoundly sombre expression. Gone the old affability! Where were his quips and oddities now?

The main causes of the Australian defeat, as

THE DEFEAT AT EASTBOURNE

it seemed to the writer, were fielding just as brilliant as the Australians' own, captainey that put every fieldsman in the proper place, and clever spin bowling. As one watched the Ashtons, fleet of foot, sure of grasp, one thought of the heavy, plodding wanderings of England's Test match outfielders. And as one saw MacLaren move his men here and there by the most deliberate yet the gentlest waves of the hand—gestures telling of a perfectly composed mind—one thought of Douglas's volubility as he sought to obtain a tactful disposition of *his* men. There was, indeed, a tincture of bitterness in the sweet as one watched the afternoon proceed to its superb consummation.

The bowling of Gibson and Faulkner in the Australian second innings was just of that kind Australian batsmen have never really mastered. Barnes could put even Trumper at his mercy by the ball that broke away from the bat after pitching somewhere near the leg and middle stumps. Both Gibson and Faulkner exploited this dangerous ball this afternoon and by excellent fortune they both managed also a capital length. The Australians did not again find Falcon troublesome, though he bowled not a bit below his Saturday's form. Fast and fast-medium bowling, right arm, that comes more or less straight through, is the stuff Australian batsmen thrive on. They waxed fat on Howell, Douglas, Jupp and Parkin (when he bowled fast). To these bowlers they could play forward confidently. Even the slow-medium off-break rarely troubles an Australian batsman. He commonly is good at leg-side play and can get back to the wicket and force the ball away in the spin's direction. The ball that pitches on the wicket and breaks away he has never mastered. One might add, what batsmen have? This delivery demands the most discreet use of the "two-eyed stance," of back play supported judiciously by the pads. And though the Australians can play back cleverly enough on slow wickets, back play is not so much in the blood of them that they can play back easily on a fast wicket.

The finger spin used by Faulkner and Gibson to-day is to be tackled safely only by the perfect back-play technique employed, say, by Taylor, the South African, against Barnes, a year or two ago. Armstrong's struggles with Faulkner were pathetic; he merely lunged at the ball when it was in the air, lost it as it spun, then desperately changed his stance at the last minute. Bardsley played forward beautifully to the ball that bowled him, and had it come through straight he would have hit it. The ball spun several inches on pitching, and Bardsley had no pads there as a second line of defence. A lot of abuse has been hurled at the "two-eyed stance" this summer, and rightly, since too often has it been exploited against fast bowling. But, as this afternoon's Australian batsmanship has shown, there is not much hope against a ball spinning away at a good length if one uses the old-time lunge forward.

But the impressions of this glorious match likely to last longest are of MacLaren. One will see him,

THE DEFEAT AT EASTBOURNE

white-haired and beautifully calm, standing in the slips beckoning a man to a more judicious place in the field. One will see him plucking at his trousers' knees in the old way, hitching them up before he slightly bends into the classic slip position. One will see him moving across the pitch at the over's end, taking now and then one of his bowlers by the arm and giving him a word of encouragement and advice. And if these impressions should fade in a while, surely one will never forget his walk to the pavilion at the game's end, the crowd pressing round him and cheering—MacLaren with his sweater over his shoulders, his face almost lost in the folds of it, looking down on the grass as he moves for good from the cricket field, seemingly but half aware of the praisegiving about him, seemingly thinking of other times.

Scores :—

ENGLAND XI

First Innings.		Second Innings.	
G. N. Foster, c Gregory, b Macdonald	5	c and b Macdonald	11
G. A. Faulkner, b Armstrong	3	c Mailey, b Armstrong	153
G. Ashton, lbw, b Armstrong	6	lbw, b Armstrong	36
H. Ashton, b Macdonald	0	lbw, b Armstrong	75
A. P. F. Chapman, b Macdonald	16	b Macdonald	11
C. T. Ashton, c Ryder, b Armstrong	1	b Macdonald	0
M. Falcon, b Macdonald	8	c and b Macdonald	17
G. E. C. Wood, lbw, b Armstrong	1	b Macdonald	2
A. C. MacLaren, b Macdonald	0	b Macdonald	5
C. H. Gibson, not out	1	not out	0
W. Brearley, b Armstrong	1	run out	0
Extra	1	Extras	16
Total	43	Total	326

A CRICKETER'S BOOK

AUSTRALIANS.

First Innings.		Second Innings.	
H. L. Collins, b Falcon	19	c H. Ashton, b Gibson	12
W. Bardsley, lbw, b Faulkner	70	b Gibson	22
C. G. Macartney, b Faulkner	24	b Falcon	14
T. J. Andrews, b Faulkner	0	b Faulkner	31
C. E. Pellew, c H. Ashton, b Falcon	1	c H. Ashton, b Gibson	16
J. Ryder, b Falcon	10	c G. Ashton, b Gibson	28
W. W. Armstrong, b Falcon	13	lbw, b Faulkner	11
H. Carter, c H. Ashton, b Faulkner	10	c C. Ashton, b Falcon	16
J. M. Gregory, not out	16	lbw, b Gibson	0
E. A. Macdonald, b Falcon	4	not out	9
A. A. Mailey, b Falcon	4	b Gibson	0
Extras	3	Extras	8
Total	174	Total	167

AUSTRALIAN BOWLING—First Innings.

	O.	M.	R.	W.		O.	M.	R.	W.
Gregory	2	0	6	0	Armstrong	8.1	4	15	5
Macdonald	10	2	21	5					

Second Innings.

	O.	M.	R.	W.		O.	M.	R.	W.
Macdonald	31	3	98	6	Ryder	5	1	11	0
Armstrong	24.5	6	74	3	Mailey	22	3	76	0
Gregory	9	0	51	0					

ENGLAND BOWLING—First Innings.

	O.	M.	R.	W.		O.	M.	R.	W.
Falcon	18.4	2	67	6	Faulkner	16	1	50	4
Gibson	14	2	54	0					

Second Innings.

	O.	M.	R.	W.		O.	M.	R.	W.
Falcon	18	2	82	2	Faulkner	5	1	13	2
Gibson	22.4	6	64	6					